Charles H. Swan

Monetary Problems and Reforms

Second Issue

Charles H. Swan

Monetary Problems and Reforms
Second Issue

ISBN/EAN: 9783337295776

Printed in Europe, USA, Canada, Australia, Japan

Cover: Foto ©Suzi / pixelio.de

More available books at **www.hansebooks.com**

Monetary Problems
and Reforms

BY

CHARLES H. SWAN, JR.

" We demand that some safe plan be adopted whereby our legal tender paper and silver and our silver certificates shall be slowly withdrawn, and gold, gold certificates, and bank notes shall gradually take their places.

" We are opposed to any currency system whereby one party to a contract has the choice of the kind of money he shall tender when the choice is denied to the other party of the kind of money he shall accept, since recent experience shows that such a system creates distrust of all money contracts."

MASS. REFORM CLUB.

G. P. PUTNAM'S SONS

NEW YORK   LONDON
27 WEST TWENTY-THIRD STREET   24 BEDFORD STREET, STRAND

The Knickerbocker Press

1897

PREFATORY NOTE.

To many it may seem superfluous at this time to inflict the public with an essay on the much-discussed money question. Such may say that after the election of November, 1896, the issue is settled, and we have nothing more to fear. The election was certainly a great victory for Sound Money, but it was not the Waterloo of fiatism. If properly used this victory may mark the turning-point and be the Gettysburg of the contest, but the victory must be followed up, and the opportunity must be seized or the country may be in a sad plight.

Yet scarcely has the echo of the shouts of victory died away, when the victors enter on a course of catering to the silver forces, and the vanquished are allowed to lead the victors on a crusade for " International Bimetallism," —a crusade which threatens to give new life and hope to the silver dogmas.

To many of the men of the present day it appears that the country has reached a crisis in its history which cannot be successfully met unless there is a forward movement for currency reform in opposition to the principles of repudiation. At such a time it is the right of every citizen to offer suggestions, and therein must rest the author's excuse for this essay. The disease, however, from which America has been suffering has also afflicted other nations to some degree, and the principles herein elaborated are designed to be applicable to all the world.

CONTENTS.

MONETARY PROBLEMS AND REFORMS.

I.

THE ORIGIN OF MONEY, REAL AND REPRESENTATIVE.

THE subject of money in its various phases is a subject that touches every individual in the community directly to a large degree, and affects his personal prosperity, often in an inverse ratio to his power to protect his interests. It is a subject, too, which, in proportion to its importance, is one of the least understood by the people at large ; or, perhaps it would be more correct to say, it was so until the present discussions on the matter opened the public's eyes and aroused a popular interest. Moreover, to a degree peculiar to itself, there exists as to this subject a feeling among those not familiar with it that it is exceptionally abstruse, technical, and involved. There is supposed to be something particularly mysterious in regard to it. This supposition is erroneous.

Everyone handles the circulating medium to some degree, and everyone is therefore interested in obtaining the most desirable money for his goods or services. What system of money will be best calculated to se-

cure to all the surest opportunity for prosperity? Many
answers have been made. A rational solution of the
problem would seem to require that one should inves-
tigate the origin and functions of money.

The origin of money will be more plainly pointed out
if we consider the functions of money and the conditions of life which give rise to the need that those functions shall be performed. If the question is asked,
"What is money for?" the most obviously natural reply for anyone is, "Money is to buy things." Probably
nine persons out of ten would hazard this reply as a
guess. This is the very basis from which we must start.

Money is to buy things. How is the buying to be
done? Smith has something that Jones would like.
Jones inquires and finds that Smith will part with it if
Jones will give in exchange something which is equally
desirable. What this shall be they can determine for
themselves. When they have determined, each goes away
satisfied, and the trade is done. The article or articles
that Jones gives may be one thing or another, but whether
a bear skin, blankets, sheep, horses, pieces of metal, or
what-not, Smith takes them because he wants them, and
it is this fact, that Smith wants them, that gives them
their value in exchange, and enables Jones to gratify his
wants by parting with them.

All trade or commerce when reduced to lowest terms
is simply a barter as between Smith and Jones. If you
can imagine a time or condition when men are so little
developed that trading is only just begun, you can well
see that it must be confined to what each man individu-
ally can spare from a more scanty stock after supplying
his immediate wants. At first each man will produce a
small surplus, and exchange it only when he feels an im-

mediate desire to enjoy the surplus product of some
other man. Thus the fisherman may stop catching fish
when he has enough for his own family, but if he desires
a better house to live in than what he now has, he may
strive to catch more fish and exchange the surplus for
building materials. But in such exchanges it will often
be difficult to make up a fair equivalent in the articles
which the parties wish immediately to use. Thus if one
man has a cow and is trying to exchange to get a horse,
he may find that no one wants to take one cow for one
horse, and two cows may be more than a fair price for
one horse. He will therefore seek to offer some other
desirable article in a quantity that shall make up the difference between the worth of the horse and the cow. It
will thus happen that some few articles of general desirability will become commonly employed as compromises
to cover differences between the two sides of exchanges.
These articles will acquire this use by reason of various
circumstances that may for the time being make them
the most convenient for the purpose, and when in the
evolution of industry some more convenient articles may
become available, they will naturally tend to be used instead ; for man will normally seek to use those methods
of business which experience may show to require the
least expenditure of energy. The man who thus accepts one of these common articles of exchange in
return for his own products or services will have a reasonable assurance that when his own wants require to be
satisfied by some special product or service of others,
there will be no great difficulty in finding someone glad
to receive these common articles to make up any differences between the products he has to offer for immediate
use and the products he wishes to secure.

When this stage has been reached, where the community in general is willing to receive the returns for a part of its industry in articles which it must re-exchange in order to enjoy those articles satisfactorily, it is but a short step to take if one says to himself : " I will exchange *all* my surplus product for these common articles of general acceptability, and I can keep them until I want some special product of my neighbor, when he in turn will be glad to take what I offer."

When things have reached this point of development. the first crude money has arisen. What article or articles may thus be employed as money will depend entirely on circumstances, and history shows that a great variety of articles has at various times and places been so employed. Our English word " pecuniary " has been traced back to the Latin " pecus," a flock or herd, and this points to a time when cattle were the chief money. Besides this, furs and farm products of various kinds have been used. Tobacco was money once in Virginia, and potatoes have been so used in this century in back country districts of New England. Blocks of salt have served as money, and shells too.

But by far the most generally used class of commodities for this purpose has been the class of merchantable metals, iron, tin, lead, platinum, copper, silver, gold, etc. Of these, the last three named have practically proved themselves the most available, for a variety of reasons. They are comparatively valuable in small quantities, they are readily worked into convenient form, and they do not deteriorate in quality by age. Each one has a special utility of its own. In most primitive times of general poverty, pieces of copper will answer all the purposes of money. A comparatively large purchase

may not require an inordinate amount of the metal, and
for the petty transactions of the poor a small piece of
copper will be more convenient than a minute piece of
silver. But as industry becomes more diversified, and
prosperity greater, larger transactions will take place,
and it will be found more convenient to use the less
bulky metal, silver. This again will tend to be displaced
in utility by gold in the enormous transactions that later
arise.

Thus far we have traced the rise of money as an article
of general acceptability in exchange, and we have referred to the fact that each individual exchange is
brought about because each party desires what the other
offers, and considers a fair equivalent given. We are
not to suppose, however, that all transactions of exchange
will rapidly take on the character of exchanges for what
we have defined as money. The system of exchanges of
products for immediate use, without the employment of
money on either side, will still continue, and by a curious
reaction will even be facilitated by the custom of using
money in many transactions, so that even in the most
advanced civilization this system, called barter, will be
found to some extent.

This added facility, above mentioned, arises from
another function, which is sometimes said to be performed by money, but which more properly may be said
to be performed by men by reference to money. This is
the comparison of values. Money is not only to buy
things, but by referring the values of two articles to the
unit of what happens to be money at the time, a comparison is made between the values of those articles. It
is thus that money is said to be the measure of values.
Measuring values, as measuring other things, is only a

comparative process. The value to be measured is compared with a value well understood, just as a length to be measured is compared with a length well understood, but there is this difference, that while length is a physical property and quite fixed in a given article, value is only a human estimate of desirability, and must be to some degree of a fluctuating nature, even as regards the same article. This estimate may vary, and probably will, somewhat with different individuals at the same time, and yet these different estimates will tend to come together in the public mind, and establish a general uniformity in one vicinity, or, in other words, a market price for a given time and place.

There is, however, a third function, commonly performed through the use of these articles which have become generally acceptable as money. This third function is the most important of all, and furnishes the occasion for all the present monetary problems and discussions. This function is that performed when money, as we have defined it, is used as the standard of contracts for future deliveries.

It must be remembered that in the primitive condition of mankind, which we have tried to picture, we have not supposed the community has been confining itself to the use of only one article, for a medium of exchange—that is, for money to buy things with. We have supposed, what we may consider a natural development, that there may be several different articles in common use, that each of these may have some peculiar fitness for certain kinds of transactions, and that buyers and sellers will in each case use what circumstances may show to be most convenient.

Suppose now that Smith has products to dispose of

and Jones wants them, but cannot to-day furnish in sufficient quantity the article which Smith will accept in exchange. In other words, Smith wishes one of the articles of general acceptability, or what we have defined as money, and Jones cannot give that to-day. However, after he and Smith have determined how much of this article he will give and Smith will take, Jones says that he can and will give Smith just that in ten days, if Smith will agree to wait. Smith may agree. Jones then takes Smith's goods, and comes under an obligation to Smith to deliver at a future day a certain article in definite amount. We have here a debt from Jones to Smith, for in economic contemplation a debt is an obligation to deliver certain goods. The debt may arise in another way; as, for instance, Jones may go to Smith, and say : " You have a plenty of article X ; give me so much, and in ten days I will give you the same amount of the same kind." Smith may agree.

In either of these arrangements between Jones and Smith, we have an obligation of indebtedness arising by act of the parties, and this obligation exists above and before any law in deriving its binding effect. Still the law must recognise the obligation in order to assure Smith that Jones shall not skulk out of his contract ; but the function of the law is to provide a remedy for violation of the contract. If a law should suddenly say " Jones must deliver twice as much as he promised," that would be an injustice to Jones, and if it should say " Jones need deliver only half of what he promised," that would be an injustice to Smith. In either event, one man's right would be handed over to the other, whereas the law should aim to do to both an even and exact justice. This is not to say that, if Jones becomes *unable* to do all he agreed, he may not sometimes be allowed to start afresh after a settlement in insolvency, but that is an exceptional circumstance.

Not only does the obligation of this indebtedness arise by act of the parties, but the determination of the article that shall be delivered in discharge also rests in the agreement of the parties, and the same grounds that would condemn a law which should increase or decrease the quantity, would likewise condemn a law which should substitute a different quality of the same article or an entirely different article.   Smith the creditor is entitled only to what the contract calls for but he is entitled to all of that in quantity and quality.

When men have become accustomed to the use of metals for the various purposes of money, it becomes of the greatest importance in exchanging the metals for other goods that the recipient of the metal shall know how much of the metal is present and what its quality is. The metals commonly used for money can be combined with less valuable metals to form alloys, and alloys of considerable difference may not differ perceptibly to the unaided senses of man.   It is therefore of great utility and convenience that some person of skill shall test pieces of the metals, and shall place on the pieces definite marks certifying to the quality of the piece, or what proportion of fine metal it contains.   If this work is done by persons who are well known in the business to the public, and in whose skill and integrity the public by experience have confidence, the pieces so marked will be received without question as to their quality.   If, further, the weight of each piece is denoted by some distinguishing mark, and each piece is made close to some one weight, another aid will be given to trade, for by simply counting the pieces in a group one may know approximately how much of the metal is present in the whole.

This operation of certifying to the fineness and weight of convenient pieces of the metals is the act of coinage. There is nothing mystical or mysterious about it. One man with skill and honesty can do it as well as another. All that is needed is the proper scientific instruments. Nevertheless it is almost always the fact throughout the world that coinage is a government monopoly. The historical reasons that led to the seizure of this function by the authorities lie, doubtless, in the temptations for improper profits by falsely certifying to the pieces and retaining the difference. The temptation was too fascinating for impecunious rulers to resist. They did not wish to protect the public from private speculations, but sought to enjoy those speculations themselves. But however reprehensible may have been the original motives of monarchs, and oligarchies that seized this monopoly from the people, its retention in government hands, when the government is honestly administered, is amply justified by the facilities a government may have for doing the work cheaper and for securing uniformity. Still this operation is not universally in government management. There are exceptions. China, for instance, uses silver for most of its larger transactions, yet this silver has not been certified by the government, but is in large pieces that have passed through the hands of private refiners, of whom there are many in that land, and who are said to do their work well.

Thus we have endeavored to trace the origin of money from its first crude beginnings, when man may use some clumsy perishable article as his money, through the period of change in which more convenient moneys will displace the less convenient by a natural selection, down to the time when metals become the usual money ; and we have examined the act of coinage as a private and as a public function.

It must not be supposed, however, that, when a community has reached the stage of uniform government coinage, though that may be a high grade of development and the most convenient arrangement it has up to that point had, it is a complete system of exchange for the most diversified industry.

When a person has a large quantity of money even in the more valuable metals it will be quite bulky and will require especial precautions for its protection against thieves. Suppose now that some few people in the community have especial facilities for caring for large quantities of precious articles, and these men are well known for honesty and trustworthiness. It will obviously be for their advantage in spreading their business relations and will protect their customers' interests, for the customers to deliver their surplus money into the hands of these tradesmen ; and receive in exchange the promise of the recipient in each case to return an equal amount of like material on demand ; in other words the customers receive the indebtedness of the tradesmen. It will soon be evident to all in the business that in order to insure their ability to deliver all they owe when it is required they do not need to keep in their strong vaults every ounce of metal they have thus received. All of their creditors will not want to be satisfied at once, and so part of the money in their possession may be put out in the operations of their business. This is not necessarily betraying their customers' interests, provided the general bulk of their business assets is kept sufficient in value to cover their obligations, and a sufficient supply of metal is held to meet the demands of the few who may need to use what they have due. So soon as this idea becomes well recognized, there will be a competition to receive money thus for mutual benefit, and tradesmen will offer inducements to their customers thus to trust them. This will usually take the form of an added amount to be paid after a given time over and above the original debt, as interest, and we have the beginnings of banking.

When the customer delivers his money to his banker, the latter may write his promise of return upon a small paper convenient to keep or to carry, and he may agree to deliver the required amount to anyone whom the customer may point out by writing on the paper. If Jones has purchased goods, and is now paying for them, it may, and probably will, occur to him that, instead of going to the banker and drawing out what he has on deposit, it will be more convenient to transfer the banker's indebtedness to the seller of the goods by transferring the paper promise the banker gave him, and, as the banker has promised to settle with anyone whom Jones may point out, the seller will be able to get the money when he needs it. If the seller does not immediately need the hard cash and *has confidence* in the banker, he will readily see the convenience of the arrangement and will probably agree. The seller may in like manner transfer the paper to his own creditor, and he again to another, until finally the paper may have passed through a hundred hands before some one needs to call on the banker for the money.

In these transactions the paper promise has been used instead of money. It represents money, and *because the business men have confidence* in its integrity, they are willing to receive it. As it represents money and passes

current the same as money in these transactions, it may
be called representative money. It has one of the uses
of the real money it represents, it has currency ; but
there is one important distinction between the real
money and the representative money. The real money
does not depend on the credit or solvency of any man
or set of men, but on the value of the commodity itself ;
while the representative money rests upon the goodness
of the promise it carries. The ultimate value of the
real money rests on the market value of itself, but the
ultimate value of the representative money rests on the
value of what it represents. The fact that Jones and
the others are willing to receive it is because they believe it is good for what it claims. Its acceptability
rests in the agreement of the parties, and in that it closely
resembles the real money.

This representative money is a crude bank-note, and
in fact the transactions of receiving money on deposit
against the paper promises of the receiver, as above described, are an outline of the process by which bank-
notes became introduced into general use in England.

The bank-notes of the previous description are issued
by a comparatively small number of men in the community, who are in that business and are generally known
to merchants. A very similar species of paper, which
may have a limited use as representative money, is a
note given for a debt by a merchant not in the banking
business. This note will be less current as representative
money, because of the limited circle of business men
who will be familiar with its credit.

There are, however, other kinds of representative
money than the bank-notes and business notes which
have just been described. The most important for large

commercial transactions is the bill of exchange. Suppose Jones owes a debt to Smith to be discharged in Jonesville, while Smith is at a distance in Smithville. It may not be convenient to travel to Jonesville to collect the debt, but if Brown, for instance, also living in Smithville owes an equal debt to be discharged at Jonesville, Smith may sell to Brown the claim against Jones by a writing directing Jones to settle with Brown, and Brown can send this written direction to his creditor in Jonesville, who will thus be able to satisfy his own demand. It is true, the creditor may refuse the arrangement, but it is so manifestly convenient for all parties, that, if the paper is really good for what it claims, he probably will acquiesce. Such paper when in proper legal form is a bill of exchange, and, so far as the credit of the parties is well known, it may be used in transactions to represent money, and thus becomes representative money.

We have seen that the banker's promissory note will circulate more readily as representative money than the promissory notes or bills of exchange of individual business men, for the reason that, while the private note or bill may be perfectly secure, the credit of the banker will be much better known. Accordingly it will be for the advantage of a business man who holds a private bill or note to exchange it for his banker's note, and pay the banker a commission for the service in the shape of interest or discount. The banker will thus be indebted *without interest* on his own notes and will hold an equal claim *with* interest against private parties. This interest will be his profit and will form the inducement for the existence of the banking business. Unfortunately, too, it will form a temptation to the banker to issue a larger quantity of his demand notes than he can safely look out for, and the very nature of his business will expose the public to peculiarly distressing and far-reaching disaster if he becomes bankrupt. Accordingly we find that the government usually places restrictions on the conduct of this business, and the issuing of these notes. Often the latter function is reserved to specially incorporated banking companies, or banks, which by controlling a larger capital are better able to succeed than a private banker in the same line. The restrictions which at various times and in different countries have been placed on banks of issue have been too numerous to mention, and have ranged from what is practically no restriction, to the most rigid cast-iron rules. It must not be supposed, however, that the issuing of promissory notes is the sole or chief function of banks, even in relation to representative money. Fully as important in utility and magnitude is the receiving of deposits, subject to be repaid on demand or on presentation of checks, which are a form of bills of exchange. These deposits are, within safe limits, loaned out to business men on good security, and the processes of commerce are thereby facilitated. The checks drawn against such deposits form a very convenient and acceptable substitute for real money, and are therefore a species of representative money.

The profits of bank-note issues *seem* so certain and the risks of the issuer so slight, that there is a very seductive inducement to the authorities to secure some of those profits directly to the government. It is not unknown that a government sometimes issues its own demand notes, and encourages their use as representative money. Such issues are unfortunately usually complicated with other matters, and so do not stand on their own merits, but they are quite generally condemned by conservative financiers. Still a general condemnation might in particular instances be unjust. In general it may be said that the government, not loaning money, must put out its notes by making purchases with them, and that as this output cannot of necessity be governed by the requirements of trade, the government is less fitted to regulate the amount issued than are banking companies. In other words, the government is doing only one wing of the banking business, and is under the constant strain of standing ready to redeem its notes. Still a government note issue may possess what is to the common people a great advantage, namely, uniformity, and in special cases may be excusable. For instance, it appears to be true that a questionable bank can best float its notes when they are in notes for small values, because small notes are largely available for transactions with the poor, who, from their ignorance of a bank's credit, are less able to protect their interests by recognizing and rejecting the poorer notes. Accordingly most governments place an inferior limit below which their banks are not allowed to issue notes. If now it seems desirable at a given time to have small notes in general use, it may well be argued that a *limited* amount of such notes if issued by the government, well secured by provisions for immediate redemption, will better protect the poor, and not clog the course of business. If at any time less circulating medium is required, the reduction can readily take place at the top by withdrawals of the larger notes of the banks.

The last, and to the poor man the most important, kind of representative money to be particularly discussed is small-change tokens. When, in the evolution of industry, the article in commonest use as money is a metal of considerable value in a small piece, as, for instance, silver, it will still be necessary often to deal with values smaller than can conveniently be offset against a veritable piece of money metal, for the piece will be too small. A need at once arises for a representative money to serve in the place. This need is frequently met by taking a piece of baser metal of less value than the diminutive money to be represented, and stamping on it a mark importing that the person or persons issuing it will receive it in business at its representative value, or, when a large quantity of such pieces is presented, will redeem them in standard money. These tokens, if not in excess of the needs of business, and if issued by reliable parties, will circulate at their representative value, which does not depend on the amount of metal present, as in the case of a piece of real money, but on the credit of the issuer ; though, of course, the presence of the metal is a guaranty to the extent of the value of the metal.

These tokens are in effect promissory notes, and like paper notes may be issued by private parties or by the government. Practically it is almost everywhere a government function, and its limitation as such seems to be justified on the same grounds as might justify small government notes on paper, as above explained—namely, to secure uniformity, and protect the poor from impositions. In lands where silver constitutes the chief money, it is customary to have tokens of copper or nickel alloys ; and in lands where gold is the chief money, in addition to copper and nickel tokens there are usually silver tokens also.

The circulating medium may thus be classified :

a. Real Money.

b. Representative Money $\begin{cases} \text{Private Notes,} \\ \text{Bills of Exchange,} \\ \text{Bank-Notes,} \\ \text{Checks,} \\ \text{Government Notes,} \\ \text{Tokens.} \end{cases}$

II.

FIAT MONEY; LEGAL TENDER.

It has been pointed out how money originates as a system or method of supplying certain wants felt by the community, and how this is brought about by individuals who, in seeking to conduct business in a convenient way, become familiar with the use of certain articles as temporary possessions which they will generally have to dispose of in order to reap the result of industry. Attention has been called to the fact that the use of such articles as mediums of exchange, and to serve all purposes of money, is a customary use growing out of the agreements of many different individuals each in pursuit of his own profits. The acceptance of such articles in direct exchange is because each party has bargained for and received what he is disposed to consider a fair equivalent in general. The further use of money as a measure of values is also a matter of habit. The custom of comparing values by referring them to the articles commonly received in exchange is merely a matter of convenience. There is no essential reason why values *must* be compared with the medium of exchange. So, too, when two persons are bargaining for a future delivery of some article, the fact that the article finally selected happens to be used as a medium of exchange does not affect the economic nature of the transaction.

From an economic point of view there can be no difference between an obligation to deliver what happens to be a medium of exchange and an obligation to deliver some other article. In either event the selection has been made by the agreement of the parties, and the obligation is as to a certain quantity of a certain thing. It is thus that we may say that in *economic contemplation* any obligation to deliver specified goods is a debt. It would seem that the obligation made by the agreement of the parties should be altered only by the agreement of the parties. It would seem further that the obligation should not be altered indirectly by changing the definition of terms used in the agreement. Nor should the fact that the law looks on a debt for money in a different light from the way in which it looks on a debt for other goods, make any difference as to impairing the obligation.

If the circulating medium is silver, and a certain weight of silver is known as a *quod*, then an obligation for one hundred quods is just as much an obligation for a certain amount of silver as if the word silver were specified and the weight told in ounces. If a law steps in and alters the amount or quality of silver or gives the word *quod* a new meaning in that contract, then an injustice is done to one party or the other. Either the one is obliged to give more than he agreed ; or, the other is obliged to rest with less than was promised him.

It may, perhaps, be said that the government has a right and duty to define the monetary unit, but the act of applying a name to a definite amount of metal, so that that name when used in subsequent transactions shall have that meaning, is very different from declaring in effect that the new meaning shall apply to existing con-

tracts, in which the term had a distinctly different meaning in the contemplation of the parties at the time the
contract was made.

In spite however of everything above said, it is nevertheless true that no despotic power of government in
disregard of property has been oftener or more universally
employed than this power of tampering with contracts ;
and that, too, not only by governments professedly despotic, but even by those claiming to be actuated by the
principles of justice and liberty. It would sometimes
seem as if the louder the protestations of liberty and
justice to all, the more determined a government may be
in a tyrannous course of intermeddling with private
affairs.

The state of mind that can give rise to a belief in the
rightfulness of a law declaring something a legal tender
on a contract, which is of less value than the contract
calls for, is an enigma probably impossible of solution.
It would seem to be based, however, on a confusion between the moral duty of a contract and the *remedy* for a
contract or that which gives the contract the assurance
of fulfilment. The duty of a contract rests on the innate
sense, that a man ought to perform, to the best of his
ability, what he has promised. The remedy for a contract is the recognition which the law gives to the duty.
Unfortunately, too many men are desirous of escaping
from the performance of their contracts, and while the
duty of a contract may be said to be before and above
the law, without a remedy it is valueless in commercial
transactions. The creditor, therefore, is utterly at the
mercy of the debtor until the law steps in and recognises
the duty, and gives a remedy for the enforcement of the
debt. Now as the creditor's power to avail himself of

the benefit of the debt depends on, and is limited by, the remedy which the law allows, by a confusion of ideas it may be supposed that the creditor's *right* to a remedy is simply what the law graciously gives. If once this step is taken we have no assignable limit within which the law must refrain from meddling, and we are launched on the turbulent sea of legal-tender enactments.

One of the earliest and crudest forms of legal-tender laws is an act tampering directly with the standard coinage. Suppose, as in the case mentioned, the unit of money is a definite quantity of silver called a *quod*, and the prince or legislature exacts that a piece of silver of only three quarters of the weight of the quod shall be a legal tender for a quod. Obviously the creditors on existing contracts are helpless, and must receive the little quod or nothing for the big quod promised. Equally obvious it should be that buyers and sellers will receive the little quod, in immediate exchanges, only for its market value, and there will then be a big quod and a little quod, of different purchasing power, in use in the same place at once. Practically, the same result is reached if one of the old quods is made a legal tender for one and one third quods. Instead, however, of making a little quod by weight or giving a higher name-value to an existing piece of metal, the prince may make the new quod of the same weight as the old one, but with an increase of the baser alloy present. This accomplishes the same result; and has this advantage that the new quod looks like the old, so that the people are more readily deceived.

These, then, are the three ways of debasing the standard coin of a country :—either, to reduce the weight of the piece, and make the reduced piece a legal tender for the old piece ;—or, to coin the same pieces as before, but decree that each shall be a legal tender on existing contracts for more than its old name implied ;—or, to coin pieces of the same weight as before but of a reduced fineness and to make them legal tender with the old. However, it is not at all unusual to find that when one of these methods is employed in a scheme of debasement, the others are also associated with it. Debasement, properly speaking, refers simply to applying the old name to a lesser amount of metal, and in order to effect an impairing of contract rights must be accompanied by a legal-tender law, for otherwise creditors would not receive the smaller coins for more than their market value as stamped metal, but the act of debasement is so universally poisoned with this legal-tender law, that the term *debasement* is generally used to cover both operations. This matter of debasement in its broad sense is frequently glossed over and condoned by the title of seigniorage, and many economic writers assert that if a slight seigniorage is imposed, only covering the cost of minting, the reduced coins will circulate equally and at the same values as the unreduced coins.

This is not the place to discuss the correctness of this assertion in fact. It is enough to say that if a coin has hitherto contained one hundred grains, and an equal tender coin of ninety-nine grains is put out, there is at once an invitation to holders of the older full-weight coins to abstract the one grain, and this invitation will in longer or shorter time have the effect of reducing the whole circulation to ninety-nine-grain pieces. However, whether the views of seigniorage advocates are correct or not is aside from the question at issue. To decree a ninety-nine-grain piece to be legal tender on existing contracts for the hundred-grain piece must result in this, that the creditor will only get ninety-nine grains where he is entitled to one hundred, and this is the injustice against which complaint is being made. If it at any time seems to be desirable to charge a seigniorage of one per cent., for instance, a proper and just way will be to coin one hundred full-weight pieces and deliver ninety-nine of them to the person depositing the metal, rather than to deliver one hundred pieces of only ninety-nine grains each. The depositor receives the same metal in either arrangement, but, if the pieces are full-weight pieces, creditors are protected.

Another class of legal-tender laws deserves to be mentioned here. It is that class of laws providing for what is variously called a "least current weight," or "limit of tolerance." These laws are designed not to enrich the prince or state or primarily to defraud, but are supposed to be a protection to trade, from the reasonable wear and tear to which coins are subjected. Such a law will provide that so long as a coin has not lost a certain small proportion of its standard weight it shall be legal tender as if of full weight. On theory there would seem to be no reason for forcing a creditor to accept short weight, even if resulting from reasonable wear, but in practice the amount of injustice accomplished by this class of laws is, comparatively with the injustice of general legal tender, so slight that it is not much considered, though such laws must be an invitation to rub the coins down as near to the limit as possible.

The method above described for tampering with the money of a country, namely, to debase the coins in weight, fineness, or nomenclature, and apply legal-tender laws, is so barefaced and self-evident a fraud, that it is almost universally denounced, and it is of late years seldom used by a civilized government. There is, however, another method by which the same nefarious end can be attained under the plausible pretext of "regulating the value of money"—as if money needed any other regulation than to be let alone to find its own market level. This idea of regulating the value of money has its enthusiastic advocates in all countries of the present day, and has permeated to individuals in all classes of society. It is based on the idea that the order of the government, the fiat of law, gives money its basic value. It is therefore called the doctrine of fiatism, and money that is tainted with this idea is called fiat money.

The idea is put into practice somewhat thus : Suppose again the unit of money is a certain amount of silver called a "quod," and that the business community has made many contracts calling for the delivery of quods. Each of the contracts has been made on the faith and credit of the quod as a definite amount of silver. At this point the law steps in and says that an arbitrary amount of some other substance shall be a legal tender for every quod due. If the market value of this new article is greater per nominal quod than the market value of silver per quod, of course no debtor will avail himself of his "privilege" to give something better than he owes, but if the market value of the new thing is less than that of silver, of course debtors will take advantage of the fact and pay their debts in the cheaper new money. It would seem to be obvious that, in thus forcing a creditor to take a new article different from the one contemplated by the name used when the contract was made, or otherwise to lose the debt, the law is just as unwarrantably interfering with the sacredness of contracts, as when it forces a creditor to rest with a smaller amount than promised of the identical article promised.

This method of using legal-tender laws is sometimes applied to bulky commodities, sometimes to another metal, and sometimes to the paper promises to pay the standard metal, but the vicious principle is the same in either case, namely, the forced discharge of a contract by delivery of something other than that demanded by the contract. The first case, that of bulky commodities, is very rare and found only in sparsely settled countries, but the last two are unfortunately too common. The second case occurs generally when silver is the standard money, and the law steps in to make a less valuable piece of gold a legal tender on existing contracts, or when gold is the standard money, and the law steps in to make a less valuable piece of silver a legal tender on existing contracts. In either event there is the same injustice done. There is nothing in either silver or gold that makes either act better than the other. The third case put is that of paper promises to pay. Instead of requiring a substantial thing in payment, this law allows the creditor to be put off with the mere promise of a third party subject to all the fluctuations or losses which that party's credit may suffer. It may be worse in degree, but in principle there is no difference between this substitution of a third party's credit and the substitution of an article not demanded at an arbitrary rate.

When such a law as has been described is passed, namely a law to allow the substitution of one metal for another,—the law usually fixes a definite amount of the second metal which shall go for a definite amount of the first metal, and this amount remains the same without regard to the changes in the market prices of the two metals. The ratio which exists between legally equivalent weights of the two metals is called the legal ratio of value. It is obvious that in a given case that metal which is cheaper according to the legal ratio will be used in discharging contracts and, as this will apply even to contracts made when the other metal was the circulating medium, all contracts are thus exposed to the risks of a depreciation in the metal out of circulation. The creditor never gets the benefit of a rise in either metal, but must stand the risks of depreciation in both, unless he has specifically stipulated for one particular metal. This, however, is something that many will neglect to do. Normally it would seem that the risk of depreciation should be offset by the possibility of profit from appreciation,—that he who bears one should enjoy the other, but by this system all risk falls on the creditor and all chance for profit on the debtor. It is a game of "heads I win, tails you lose";—and this distribution of risk and profit remains the same even when the market ratio of two metals may happen to be the same as the legal ratio, for, whichever way the market turns, the creditor is bound to go down.

This system is known as bimetallism. The term is rather unhappily chosen, for what it really means is that two metals shall be used as money, whereas the essential feature of what is called bimetallism is the legal-tender law which makes either metal a legal tender at a fixed ratio. It has already been pointed out that in the evolution of industry two or more metals may come to be used as money for different kinds of transactions without the assistance or interference of law. Under such circumstances the metals will circulate at their market values from time to time. Such a system of two metals

would seem to be what should be meant by the term
"bimetallism." That term, however, has become twisted
into the name of the legal-tender system above described,
which would be more accurately named, by the term
" alternate tender system " sometimes also applied to it.
The basis of the system rests in the fiat theory of money,
the idea that it is the right and duty of the law to interfere
in the private money contracts of the people, and alter
them at pleasure.

That such a right should be claimed and exercised by
a *despotic prince* is only natural, but that any government
claiming to be actuated by principles of justice and
liberty should consider such a course, not only justifiable,
but even commendable, is a most remarkable phenome-
non. Yet at the present day there is a certain class of
people who consider opposition to bimetallism as evi-
dence of the rankest kind of monarchical sympathies,
and consider the principles of bimetallism as inherently
a part of the theory of popular government. That a
principle so despotic can be regarded as essentially
democratic is most extraordinary.

The discussions of bimetallism have mostly been waged
along the line of its expediency, but this is not the
place to go into that field. It would seem, to be sure,
that a system founded on the idea, that a creditor has no
rights which the government is bound to respect, must
necessarily frighten capitalists, and impede the free dis-
posal of capital, without which no secure prosperity is
possible. The idea, however, which it is desired to em-
phasize here is the inherent injustice of such a system,
and that should be a sufficient condemnation.

The disciples of the bimetallic creed do not agree
among themselves as to what is the proper application of

the system. They may be grouped as national and international bimetallists. The national bimetallists wish any one great nation, particularly the United States, to pass their pet law and see whether the market ratio will become the same as the legal ratio, so that the two metals gold and silver shall be at a " parity." The international bimetallists cry out against this. They say it would be wrong if tried by one government at a ratio differing from the market ratio, but if tried by all the leading nations it would be all right. In either case no desire is shown to start the system on the market ratio. Both national bimetallists and international bimetallists are entirely ready to expose existing creditors to the risk of a fifty-per-cent loss, and insist on the absurd ratio about one half of the present one in the market.

The alternate tender or bimetallic system supposes in its completeness that both metals are freely coined for all comers, but as this exposes the coins to the fluctuations in the market ratios, an apparent bimetallism as a compromise has often been established. In this scheme one of the metals is limited in its coinage to government account and less than the face value of the metal is used, Provision is then made for a direct or indirect redemption of the coins so that they shall circulate at their face values. Besides this they are often limited in legal tender to some small sum. In such a scheme the inferior coins so bolstered up may circulate at par, but it is obvious that they do not do so on the value of the metal. It is rather on the credit of the government, and as the government by its legal-tender enactment has put them out at full value it is under an obligation to see that they stay at full value, and, if necessary to that purpose, to redeem them in standard metal. As they are an obligation or debt of the government and depend for full value on the government's credit they are only tokens or representative money, and this is so without regard to whether they are full legal tender or only limited legal tender. The making of metallic credit money legal tender is no different in theory from making paper credit money legal tender. In either case the creditor gets instead of the real monetary metal the credit of a third party, and the fact that in one case there is present a valuable metal to the extent of part of the obligation can make no difference except so far as it may or may not be considered an added security.

The token coinage of most, probably all, countries is made a legal tender to a limited amount, but this is so generally protected by strict limitations on its issue, and provisions for redemption direct or indirect that it usually circulates at par. Still, as it rests in part on credit, there is a possibility of extraneous depreciation, and on principle it seems improper to throw even that risk on creditors.

So too, when notes, or paper credit money, are made legal tender, there is sometimes a provision for redeeming them so that for a time, and it may be a long time, they circulate at par, but nevertheless there is still the possibility of depreciation, and the risk of that is thrown on the creditor. Of this nature are the United States greenbacks since 1879. The notes of the Bank of England are, apparently to be classed here, but in reality their legal-tender quality is modified by the provision that they are legal tender only so long as the bank redeems them in gold. Thus the legal-tender power ceases to operate as soon as it becomes dangerous, while the greenback remains legal tender in spite of dangerous circumstances.

Many persons will recognize at once the hardship

which a legal-tender law throws on creditors, but will
say that the creditor as a rule is a grinding master, rich
and heartless, and not deserving of much consideration
beside the poor debtor, who is a much-abused fellow.
The creditor is taken to be essentially bad, while indebtedness is considered almost a virtue. It would not be
difficult to show, as has often been done that this view is
entirely erroneous in fact ;—that the creditor as a class
is more apt to be a poor person unable to protect himself to any degree, and the debtor is as likely as not a
wealthy individual or rich corporation ; that the bulk of
creditors are the poor who have laid up a small invest-
ment, or widows and orphans who are dependent on
what is due them, or laboring men waiting for their
weekly wages, while the rich debtor is well able to protect his own interests. All this might easily be shown,
but it is really aside from the direct point, which is that
even and exact justice should be done to *both* debtor *and*
creditor.

When an honest man becomes bankrupt, it is right to
relieve his necessity by a bankrupt law, nor does that
neglect the creditor, for the creditor's interest then is to
get what he can before worse happens. A legal-tender
law, however, which makes less an equivalent for more,
takes no account of any man's *ability* to fulfil his contracts, but with one fell swoop strikes a horizontal reduction of debts for all alike, and is in effect a universal
bankrupt act. When it is said, as sometimes is, that a
legal-tender law is necessary to avoid bankruptcy, such a
law is, in reality not an escape from bankruptcy, but the
most emphatic confession of bankruptcy.

It is appalling to consider the amount of injustice that
even in enlightened lands has been done to the helpless

through this insidious proceeding. The fortunes of the rich have been swept away as by a cyclone, and the hard earned savings of the poor have melted into nothing.

And the worst of it all is that the perpetrators of these things are often, yes, usually, in the main, honest, well meaning men, who suppose they are acting for the good of the public. Among the wrongs done in Liberty's name legal tender must hold a prominent place. It seems to be almost a mania to rush to legal tender in any public crisis. At the very time when business confidence is most needed, the most deadly blow is struck at that confidence. The apologists of legal-tender paper will tell you that in times of public need gold and silver are cowards, are hidden away, and only the paper is left. These people forget to inform you that gold and silver are not persons, but disappear because bad laws have forced out unreliable paper, and have threatened the owners of the metals with unnecessary losses, so that the owners are only taking proper measures for their own safety when they secure their gold and silver.

If such laws were passed only by those recognized as scheming, unscrupulous self-seekers, it would be comparatively easy to combat them. The mere statement of the villany would be enough to rouse public indignation to a point where such laws would be impossible. But when really honest men honestly believe them right, it is doubly hard to persuade the trusting people that its trusted leaders are wrong.

Many a man deplores the dangers and wrongs of legal-tender laws, but believes such laws are necessary. The reasons which may induce men to consider these laws necessary may be roughly grouped as due to two causes. First, a desire to introduce some new kind of money ;

and second, a belief that money needs these laws in order to circulate and pay debts. The first cause may be treated very briefly. If in the evolution of simpler forms of business, a new kind of money becomes convenient, the business community will not need any forcing to make use of what is really convenient, and if it is not really convenient then it should not be forced. A proposition may be raised to issue certain paper money, for instance. Paper that is so well secured for payment, and so thoroughly reliable that it possesses the confidence of business men, is so manifestly convenient that it will readily be accepted in all kinds of transactions *without the intervention of a law;* whereas if it is not so reliable as to have the confidence of business men, that is a sufficient reason why it should not be forced upon them. Such poor paper should not be issued. Again,— the lawmakers may believe that there is not enough of one metal to supply the needs of trade, and so may think it necessary to make two metals legal tender at a fixed ratio. If the government simply stamps coins of both metals, that is a perfectly harmless proceeding, and business men can use either or both, as they find convenient ; but, if they do *not* find both convenient, that is the very best reason in the world why the undesired metal should not be forced upon them. The desire, then, to introduce a new kind of money, contrary to the convenience of the business world, is not a legitimate desire.

The second cause for believing legal-tender laws necessary is found in a more or less conscious belief in the fiat theory of money,—that money needs these laws in order to circulate and pay debts. This involves an examination of the three uses of money in their relation to legal tender,—namely, money as used to buy things, money as the measure of values, and money as the standard of contracts for future deliveries, that is, debts. It has been pointed out that real money is some valuable article generally desired, and representative money is a claim for real money ; also, that, in the transaction of buying and selling, the seller accepts the buyer's money because he considers it a fair equivalent. The seller will not give up his goods till sufficient money is offered him to be a fair equivalent, and if a legal-tender law applies a given name to an article only half as valuable as that which formerly bore it, then the seller will, when he discovers the fraud, call for money of a proportionately higher name than before, but still in actual value equivalent to the goods sold. If the money put forth by law is utterly worthless, trade will be crippled or reduced to primitive barter, but the habit of using whatever is put forth is so generally convenient that, unless the money is positively vile, trade can manage somehow.

Thus both buyer and seller are in a position to discount a legal-tender law, except through their own ignorance, which will soon be enlightened by the example of their shrewder comrades. The circulation of money, then, needs no such laws.

The second use of money is even more unembarrassed by legal tender. This second use is the comparison of values, and is entirely a customary mental process. No law can say that a man shall not estimate his possessions as equal in value to stated portions of whatever he chooses to compare them with.

The real rub comes in regard to the third use of money, namely as a standard of debts. In this connection it is often said that there need to be legal-tender laws in order

2

that the debtor may know how to discharge his debt ; but how is this? A debt in economic contemplation is an obligation by contract for the delivery of specified goods. The obligation arises by agreement of the parties, and the article to be delivered is named by them. Is anything more needed ? If Smith has contracted to deliver one hundred pounds of butter to Jones, does Smith need an act of legal tender to tell him what he must deliver ? Is it not perfectly obvious that a delivery of what is named in the contract is the evident and only fulfilment of the contract ? The principle does not change if the contract calls for a certain quantity of a metal. If Smith has contracted to deliver a certain weight of silver of a certain quality, is not that amount of silver the full and only performance of the contract ? Can it make any difference, if Smith and Jones by language they both understand have called this certain quantity of silver by the name " one hundred quods "? The performance or fulfillment of the contract to deliver goods is the delivery of the very goods specified ; nothing more ; nothing less. A sufficient tender on such a contract is the performance carried as far as it may be without the acceptance of the performance by the creditor. What this sufficient tender is, is, therefore, pointed out by the terms of the contract, which designate the performance. This tender and *only* this tender should be recognized by the law as a LEGAL *tender*, or a sufficient tender in law on the contract.

It may be said that this is true as a general statement, but will not be sufficient to cover particular facts. Let us see as to this. Let us examine the principle in connection with the various classes of legal-tender laws, those which provide for less of the metal promised, and those which provide some other less valuable metal, thing, or obligation.

Suppose, then, that a country starts fresh, with no legal-tender laws, or after abolishing its legal-tender laws. Suppose the government simply points out 23.22 troy grains of pure gold as a monetary unit, and applies a name to that unit, calling it a dollar. This meaning of the word dollar will be well understood by the business world, and whenever that word is used in contracts, it will have this definite meaning. A contract to deliver dollars will, therefore, be a contract to deliver a certain amount of gold, and the performance of that contract will be the delivery of that gold. A sufficient tender on that contract will be a tender of this full performance. There is no need for any act of legal tender. The definite amount of gold is a legal or sufficient tender on that contract by the very terms of the contract. Not only has the contract fixed the amount of a valuable commodity to be delivered, but the law has no right to intervene and say that a less amount shall do. And this intervention is entirely unnecessary. Nor should the fact that the pieces of metal used in paying this contract have lost by wear a small portion of their original weight be a reason for throwing the loss by that wear on the creditor. To be sure, if the provision for a least current weight exists when the contract is made, that operates in the definition of the term dollar used in the contract, but it is not necessary, for the matter is to be determined by weight, and when the coins are weighed it is no harder to value them at their true weight than at some arbitrary increase over that weight. Moreover, it seems to put the home creditor to a disadvantage as against the foreign creditor, for in payments made abroad the legal-tender law cannot run, and the coins will go only for their actual weight, while the home creditor must put up with the loss of the difference which the law may allow. It is only fair to say that the practical injustice from this particular kind of legal-tender laws is very small, but the purpose here is to show that even this kind of legal-tender laws is unnecessary.

In regard to the legal-tender laws which provide for the substitution of some other metal, thing, or obligation, it has already been said, but will bear repeating, that the use of several metals at the same time, and the use of representative money, which rests on some one's obligation, may often be found very convenient, but this very convenience will render such other metals and obligations readily acceptable *at their market values for the time being.* If they are convenient, no legal-tender law is needed to make them be accepted at their market values, and, if they are not convenient or trustworthy, no law should seek to force them out at an arbitrary rating.

The last kind of legal-tender laws to be considered may seem to be really necessary. This is the limited legal-tender laws which apply to small change tokens of silver, or other metals. One may say that if a contract calls for a fractional part of the gold unit, and such fractional part is too small to be paid with any gold coin, a positive enactment will be needed to say what shall be a payment. How is this? Let us suppose that the country with its monetary unit of 23.22 grains of fine gold called a dollar, has perceived the necessity of some kind of small change. Suppose that the government or private parties of well known solvency have issued obligations or tokens of paper, silver, bronze, etc., for small fractions of the dollar, and that ample provision for redemption has been made, but *no act of even limited legal tender* has been passed. The necessity that gave rise to these tokens or representative monies will cause them to circulate readily, for they will possess the confidence of the business world.

Now under these circumstances if a contract calls for a payment of a sum of dollars or fractions of a dollar too small to be made with any common gold coin, the inquiry at once arises,—is there no additional interpretation which we can put on the words of the contract which may fairly be said to be within the intention of the parties? Can it not be said that, if this payment is too small to be made in gold coin, the parties contemplated that it should be made up of some other circulating medium commonly used when the payment is made, and that a sufficient amount of this other money should be paid to be of the value of the sum due according to the market values of the monies at the time of payment? This seems a reasonable interpretation, and by it the necessity for even limited legal-tender laws for tokens is obviated, for by the terms of the contract the tokens are a valid performance of the fractional sum, and so are a sufficient tender. But this difference is to be noted, that by thus interpreting the contract, the representative money is a sufficient tender only at its market value when paid, so that the creditor gets the full value of his dues, while under a legal-tender law a fixed quantity of the representative money is designated, and any risk of depreciation is thrown on the creditor. Furthermore, the objection cannot be raised that this interpretation of the contract would open the door to allowing an unlimited legal tender of representative money, for, it is only when the sum is too small to be paid in standard metal that the reason arises for enlarging the definition of the terms used. In this connection it will be interesting to observe that, when copper token cents were first issued by the United States, nothing was said in the law about their being legal tender, even for small sums. They were simply left to circulate as conveniency might dictate, and so continued for many years.

III.

RESULT OF LEGAL TENDER AND THE REMEDY.

THE result of legal-tender laws has been that throughout the world there is a large mass of legal tender representative money which the various governments are under obligation to keep at par with its nominal value ;— a thing which the different governments in greater or less degree succeed in doing. Thus Great Britain has in round numbers about $112,000,000 of silver tokens, France has about $490,000,000 of the same kind, Germany has about $215,000,000 of such money, and the United States has some $625,000,000 of silver tokens and an additional amount of $500,000,000 of legal-tender paper. Of this burden of the United States all but about $75,000,000 of silver fractional tokens is full legal tender, and exposes the whole business of the country to losses by depreciation. The tokens of Great Britain are legal tender only for limited amounts, and are supposed to be issued only as there is a business need for them. This is the case with $110,000,000 of Germany's token silver, and with $57,000,000 of the French, but both these countries have out large quantities of full legal-tender tokens, and the United States has inflicted on itself an atrocious amount of such stuff. The German and French pieces were mostly coined in the first place as real silver money, when silver was high in price, and the pieces contained at that time full value. When silver fell these countries limited the coinage of silver, but undertook to maintain the outstanding pieces at par. This naturally threw the circulation value of the pieces on to the governments' credit by the difference between the bullion and the legal-tender value of the pieces, which thus became tokens or obligations of the governments. The effect was the same as if the governments had issued, in exchange for the coins, demand notes secured by the amount of silver bullion in the coins to be held as a metallic reserve, only, instead of issuing paper obligations and holding the metallic reserve in their own vaults, they used the reserve as the material on which to stamp the obligation, and thus each holder of an obligation held also the reserve appropriated to that particular obligation. In the United States the same result was reached, but without any such excuse. The great bulk of the silver tokens of the United States has been deliberately put out as a government speculation under the laws for purchasing silver and coining silver dollars, which are miscalled " standard " silver dollars, when in reality they are only token silver dollars.

Such a system is dangerous and clumsy in the extreme. It is dangerous in that, like all legal-tender laws, even before depreciation, it throws arbitrarily a risk upon the creditor, and thus threatens the security of all invested capital. It is clumsy for the people in that it uses a heavy, bulky material for representative money. If the people are to carry round a heavy, bulky article, they should have the satisfaction and security of knowing that they are carrying it for its own value, and not as a mere representative. On the other hand, if the government wishes to devote that amount of bulky silver to the purpose of a reserve, it can protect itself better by issuing non-legal-tender paper against it. The paper will be no better and no worse than the tokens for security, but it will be more convenient for the people, and the government will be able to take advantage of all increase in the market value of the reserve. The government will in either case be bound to make up any loss by depreciation of the reserve, but in the case of tokens it cannot take advantage of all gains ; for if the value of the material of the tokens, which is here considered as a reserve, rises above the face value of the tokens, the holder of the tokens will reap the benefit, not the government.

Besides this great mass of silver tokens the United States has a large amount of legal-tender treasury notes, issued at first in war times, and since increased by subsequent legislation. Since 1879 these notes have in fact been redeemed in gold on demand, but the law requires their constant reissue in Treasury disbursements without any regard to the needs of business, so that the redemption of the notes does not at all relieve the government of the burden of supporting them. The same may be said of the silver dollars, which, by being received for taxes and government dues, are in effect redeemed for their face value, but are immediately counted as part of the government's assets subject to be paid out or reissued, so that neither species of redemption, the direct by paying gold on demand, or the indirect by receiving for taxes lessens the government's burden. This process of reissue after redemption goes marching right straight on, without regard to any needs of business to use these notes and tokens, and, up to very recently, the number of tokens was constantly being augmented by new issues in anything but homœopathic doses. Every month Business had to open its mouth wide and swallow its allotment of so many silver pellets. Business naturally protested, and finally its stomach showed unmistakable signs of nausea. Not till then was the dosing stopped, and then only in the face of an attempt to work off the stock in trade of the silver drug upon the poor victim. The constant increase of these two kinds of legal-tender money, silver tokens, and treasury notes naturally alarmed the business world, for no government's credit, or financial potentiality, is illimitable, and a strong fear was felt that the government would be obliged to let this great mass of representative money depreciate. That would mean a loss to all creditors, and a reduction of all invested capital. The existence of this legal tender representative money was a menace to creditors and investments, and its constant increase was an added menace ; —to say nothing of the national dishonor of failing to maintain this stuff at par ; for the government by its legal-tender laws had pushed this stuff out, and had brought it about that every holder had given value equal to the face value of this legal-tender money, so that the government was under obligation to maintain it all at par, and this involved a redemption in gold when required. To fail would be national dishonor.

It is sometimes said that the silver dollars are "standard" money, because they are full legal tender. In reality they are tokens, for that very reason. Because they are made a legal-tender for a gold value more than the value of the silver, and because the government by its law has put them out at a fictitious value, it is under obligation to redeem them at that value. They are thus obligations stamped on metal, and fulfil the definition of tokens.

As the silver dollars and treasury notes of all kinds were alike mere representative money, and required to be redeemed ultimately in gold, attention was drawn to the supply of gold which the government had for the purpose, and it was found that, in the face of the constant increase of obligations, no provision was made for increasing the gold reserve. To be sure, there was a nominal increase of *metallic* reserve by the deposit of vast masses of silver bullion, but under the law this could be used in redemption only in one way, namely, to coin it into short weight token silver dollars in exchange for paper ; but this was only to exchange one demand obligation for another, and was no real redemption. There was no provision for giving a gold dollar's *worth* of silver, even, in exchange for a dollar note, and no provision for selling the silver to get the actual gold. So the whole strain was thrown on the insufficient gold stock, and the silver bullion was useless, and worse than useless : for the fear that it might be used in the only way the law allowed added to the dismay. The panic of 1893 was the natural and inevitable result. It was followed as a necessity by the repeal of the silver purchase law, and the injection of legal-tender poison was stopped. It was only the injection, however, that was stopped. No provision was made for withdrawing the poison already in the arteries of business. That was left to pollute the commercial system, and the reissue of notes and tokens after receipt or redemption went merrily on.

With a curious fatuity the very men who had led the country into this condition insisted that a further dose of the same medecine was needed, and demanded that the mints of the country should be thrown open to the free and unlimited coinage of legal-tender silver at a ratio that would put about one half of a gold dollar's worth of silver into the silver dollar. The proposition in effect was that when the government was struggling to maintain a *limited* amount of token silver at par, it should relieve itself of that burden by assuming the impossible task of maintaining an *unlimited* amount. Others have gone even further, and have demanded that, as the chief civilized countries of Europe and America have involved themselves under the same kind of burden of legal-tender token silver, they should all join in one grand game of repudiation by unitedly opening their mints to the free coinage of legal-tender silver at a ratio of only fifty per cent of its market value. It is hardly a necessity to say that the present writer is heartily against both these schemes of national or international bi-metallism, based as they are on legal-tender laws in utter disregard of the rights of creditors.

The legal-tender silver and legal-tender notes are, however, present with us both in America and other countries, and the problem in all lands is, how to deal with them without endangering creditors' rights and invested capital, or causing a shock to business. It will be a difficult matter to make any reform, for even among those opposed to opening the mints, either nationally or internationally, to the free coinage of legal-tender silver, there is much inertia. Many will say that the present silver tokens are dangerous, but that we have them, and we may as well keep all that we can keep without destroying our credit. In other words, as we have rashly approached a precipice, we must not retreat, but must stay as close to it as we can without going over the brink.

In order to arrive at any satisfactory solution of the

problem, it is necessary to have a clear idea of the ultimate end to be attained. The writer trusts that in the
preceding pages he has clearly brought out the following
ideas, that money when reduced to lowest terms depends
on the confidence of the business community ; that this
confidence is best secured when business men are free to
do business with the kinds of money they prefer ; that
the precious metals are generally most acceptable as real
money, or the ultimate measure of transactions ; that
the precious metals are normally accepted for what they
are worth in the market as valuable commodities ; that
for the purpose of facilitating the process of determin-
ing the quantity and quality of a given piece of metal,
the government stamps the metals according to some
well understood system ; that this stamping or certifying
to the weight and fineness is called coining, and for the
sake of uniformity may be justified as a monopoly ; that
as the sole function of coinage is to certify to the goodness of the metal, the government has no right to attempt
to put a fictitious value on the pieces by legal-tender
laws ; that legal-tender laws are unjust in practice, and
unjustifiable in theory, either as to their utility or necessity ; that the common law of contracts is amply sufficient to protect both parties in the discharge of a money
contract when disentangled from legal-tender laws. Furthermore, it has been admitted that credit-money or representative money is needed, but it is claimed that its
issue can best be conducted by banks, properly restricted,
to be sure, for security, but at the same time able to re-
spond to the requirements of business ; though it is freely
admitted that for certain purposes, as in small transactions, where the poor and ignorant are especially concerned, for the sake of uniformity and to protect the

poor, a *limited amount* of government credit or representative money may be desirable, and that such a case is that of small change tokens of metal or paper. It is, however, to be constantly borne in mind that this permission or opportunity for government tokens does not involve the making of them a legal tender, which is here as elsewhere bad in theory and needless in practice.

With these essential features of a thoroughly sound monetary system before us, it is not hard to point out the remedy. The only difficulty is how to attain the end. As the present lamentable condition of the representative money of the world has been brought about by the indulgence in the intoxication of legal-tender laws, the remedy seems most naturally to be the repeal of the legal-tender laws, the gradual redemption of the superfluous representative money, and the substitution of other and better forms of non-legal-tender representative money to supply the place of the present legal-tender stuff so far as is needed.

In accordance with the principles herein enunciated, a sound monetary system will provide for the free coinage of gold ; it may also provide for the free coinage of silver, and any other metals that business men may *actually* wish to use as standards, *but not at any legal-tender ratio between the metals.* Each metal will simply be stamped, under perfectly distinct names for the pieces, as to its weight and quality, and left to pass for its own market value, so that on a contract the only legally sufficient discharge or tender shall be the metal named in contract. If, then, business men see fit to draw their contracts generally for one metal in preference to another, no one can find fault, and existing debts, which have been made on the faith and credit of the gold dollar of

23.22 grains of fine gold, will be amply protected. In order that the government may not seem to throw its influence for the use of either metal in particular, it may be well to provide that the government will receive both metals indiscriminately for their market values at the time of receipt.

So much for the real money, which will, however, need to be supplemented by representative money. This should consist chiefly of bank-notes issued under some elastic system, possibly such as the well-known Baltimore Plan. The banks should, it would seem, be allowed to issue their notes either as specific silver notes or as specific gold notes, according as the needs of business may require, for it is not at all unreasonable to suppose that, with equal facilities for the use of gold and silver money, the thickly-settled centres of commerce in a country may gravitate to the gold standard, and the more sparsely settled regions of the same country to the silver standard. Besides the bank-note issues of representative money, there may properly be had a small amount of government non-legal-tender representative money, either paper or metallic tokens, of small denominations for use in making change and in petty transactions ; but this representative money, whether paper or metallic, should be strictly limited in amount with ample provisions for redemption and security against too frequent reissue.

Under this system only the metals will be legal tender, and that, too, not by force of positive enactment merely, but by force of the individual contracts themselves, and it is to be observed that this abolition of legal-tender laws will do away with the " least current weight," so that payments must be made by weight and full weight given, as is the case to-day in international transactions, where the foreign creditor gets full weight while the domestic creditor is obliged to be satisfied with short weight.

Perhaps it may be objected that the introduction, or permission for the introduction, of silver pieces to circulate only at their bullion values, as gold does, would cause confusion in trade with the silver tokens of the present time, and consequently, any possible convenience of real silver money would be overbalanced ; and the trade dollar, a coin of the description proposed, will be cited as something that was often confused with the legal-tender token silver dollar. The fact of liability to confusion cannot be denied, but the argument to be drawn from it will rather be the reverse,—namely, that if bullion silver coins and token silver coins cannot be advantageously used together, it will be better to use some other material for the needed tokens. If silver is suitable to be used as real money itself when parties so desire, it seems to be too good to serve as the mere material for representative or token money. In tokens, not the silver but the government's good credit is the basis of circulation. The silver may be worth much or little, but if the credit is good, the token may be maintained. The English shilling piece and the American silver dollar have been maintained at par over great changes in the value of the silver material. To use silver as a mere material for tokens, *if cheaper materials will do equally well*, is to lock up capital needlessly. Then will any other form of representative money do as well as silver tokens for the function which they are allowably to fulfil, namely, to furnish small change.

The only practical question will be whether the small

change representative money can best be silver, or paper
notes ; for the value of copper and nickel used in tokens
is not sufficient to raise any question concerning them.
Now as between silver tokens and *well secured* fractional
notes, for no other than well secured notes can be considered, what are the comparative advantages and disad-
vantages? In the first place the silver tokens can be
more easily counterfeited than finely engraved notes,
and at a low price for silver the counterfeit silver
pieces can be in every way as well executed as the government ones. Next, the notes will be more convenient
for the people than bulky silver tokens, as witness the
marked preference for silver certificates over silver dollars. Third, the profits to the government in either issue
of a given face value will be the same ; for either issue
is in effect a loan without interest, and the profit is the
interest on the face value put out. Fourth, it may be
said that the holder of a silver token has a pledge of
ultimate value for at least a part of the face value, by
reason of the valuable silver present, but against this
may be set the fact that this very presence of a partial
value is a strong temptation to the government to over-
issue, and make the holder depend entirely on this partial
security, and furthermore, if the silver of the token is to
be regarded as a reserve, the government is not able to
use that reserve to best advantage, for while it must be
ready to make up any depreciation in the value of the
metal, if the value rises above the face value of the
token, the holder reaps the profit. Lastly, then, how do
the expenses of a silver token coinage compare with the
expenses of a system of well secured non-legal-tender
fractional notes? The expenses of the silver tokens will
be practically represented by the loss of interest on the

first cost of the silver bullion used as the material, subject of course to be varied by rise or fall in the value of
the silver when the tokens are called in. The expenses
of the fractional notes will be practically represented by
the loss of interest on the reserve which safety may require to be kept. The expenses then of the two systems
will compare as the cost of the silver in the first instance
compares with the size of the reserve considered necessary. Now all important existing silver-token systems
were established when the price of silver was so high
that the material cost from 80 to 95 per cent. of the
face value of the tokens. The United States token
silver was first issued in 1853, and 95 per cent. approximately was the price of silver then. It is right
and almost necessary to use a high percentage of valuable material, in order to lessen the inducements for
counterfeiting. On the other hand, no one would probably maintain that anything like so large a percentage of
reserve would need to be held back of a fractional note
issue, which by the very circumstances of the case is to
be strictly limited in amount, and is, moreover, of such
a nature that business will require the greater part of it
to be kept in circulation. If the United States Government has, even with difficulty, been able to maintain at
par one thousand millions of dollars of credit money on
the confessedly insufficient reserve of 10 per cent. and
less, it would seem that for an issue of so special a nature
as is here outlined a reserve never allowed to fall below
20 per cent. would be amply sufficient.

The system of small-change money, which the writer
advocates as most convenient to the people and most
economical to the government, may be outlined as follows. An issue of non-legal-tender fractional notes re-

deemable in gold on demand, receivable for customs, taxes, and government duties,—the amount to be about the same as the present outstanding subsidiary silver, which would be withdrawn,—a special gold reserve for these fractional notes ; at the start the reserve being equal to 30 per cent. of the face value of the notes, which, when redeemed, may be reissued until the reserve has fallen to 25 per cent., when reissue must stop ; and when the reserve has fallen to 20 per cent. it must be replenished by a bond sale or revenue. At any time an additional amount of notes may be issued to anyone who wishes to deposit in the reserve their face value in gold. The difference between the 30 per cent. reserve here suggested and the 80 or 95 per cent. first cost of the silver for our tokens is considerable, and seems sufficient to justify the belief that the proposed system would be more economical than the present ; and even at the present low price of silver, which makes the silver in our tokens worth only 50 per cent, it would seem that the change to the system of notes with 30 per cent. reserve would be advantageous. To make the change now without reforming our other representative money would be but small gain, but in making a *complete* reform the tokens for small change should not be overlooked.

As a concrete application of the theory, let us note the saving that might have been made if the note system had been used instead of the token system. The token silver of the United States was first issued in 1853, and about twenty million dollars were put out in the first two years in halves, quarters, and dimes. At about 95 per cent. the cost of the silver was about $19,000,000. A 30 per cent. reserve on a fractional note issue of $20,000,000 would have been $6,000,000. The interest on the difference, namely the interest on $13,000,000 is the needless expense of the government. At 5 per cent. this interest in forty years amounts to $26,000,000, and this is the loss on only a small portion of our token out-put, and does not include the $10,000,000 of depreciation of the silver used, so that on that issue of $20,-000,000 the government has needlessly deprived itself of the benefit of $36,000,000.

The next question is how to proceed to reform our monetary system. There is a general consensus of opinion among really sound-money men that our silver system and paper money system are vicious, and that, in order to reform, we must get rid of our legal-tender notes. The writer agrees with this general opinion. The difficulty comes in regard to the plan to be adopted. Many schemes have been proposed, but they all look only to disposing absolutely of the greenbacks and Sherman notes, which are the two kinds of our legal-tender paper. Now the writer ventures to believe that the only essential step is to deprive the notes of their venom by repealing the legal-tender function of the notes on private contracts, and the provision requiring and permitting the reissue of redeemed notes. With these two insidious factors removed, the business world could be safely trusted to present the notes for redemption as fast, and only as fast, as there was no longer need for them in the channels of trade. This course too would be more feasible, for the notes are a popular form of currency, and the question whether the government should run a note-issuing business is entirely distinct from the question of having the notes legal tenders to be constantly reissued. The repeal of the legal-tender function on private contracts would *not destroy* their receivability for public dues, or prevent their being allowed as banking reserves for the national banks. The next step, and what may be the most difficult, will be to attack the vast mass of silver tokens. This mass consists, first, of about $75,000,000 of limited-tender halves, quarters, dimes, old-fashioned half-dimes, and a few twenty-cent pieces ; and, second, of perhaps $550,-000,000 of full-tender silver dollars. The circulation value of these tokens is secured by the good faith of the government as to the difference between the face value and the value of the silver as bullion. At the present price of silver the bullion in these tokens is worth about 50 per cent.; so that on the $625,000,000 of silver tokens the government's obligation is something like $300,000,000. The great bulk of the silver dollars are represented in trade by silver certificates, which are much more convenient. This fact is of importance, and furnishes an easy means for solving the problem of getting rid of the tokens. Some such provisions as the following may, then, be enacted,—A system of non-legal-tender fractional notes for twenty-five and fifty cents, receivable for government dues such as has been above outlined, shall be established. On and after a certain date in the future the present fractional silver tokens shall cease to be legal tender, but from and after the passage of the act, and, for a time running, perhaps, one year beyond the date when they cease to be legal tender, the government shall receive them at face value for all dues or in exchange for the new fractional notes and, for the convenience of foreign holders, United States Consuls abroad may be authorized to receive them in exchange for drafts on the Treasury at government expense ; from the bullion contained in the tokens thus received by the government a sufficient quantity shall be sold to provide a special gold reserve of 30 per cent. for the fractional notes issued, according to the plan heretofore outlined. The remainder of the bullion will be held with other bullion in the Treasury for purposes hereafter mentioned. On the same day when the fractional tokens cease to be legal tender absolutely, the silver-dollar tokens shall cease to be legal tender for more than sixty cents apiece, and then only in sums not exceeding sixty dollars of gold value ; but for a limited period thereafter the government shall receive them at the old rate of one dollar each for all dues, or in exchange for silver certificates, and all silver dollars which may need to be paid out in the meantime shall, to prevent frauds on the government, be surcharged with a plain stamp, and be paid and received by the government for only sixty cents each. Silver certificates shall be redeemed in the silver tokens at the new rate, so that for every nominal dollar demanded by the paper a dollar's-worth of the tokens at the new rate will be paid. Thus for certificates of the nominal value of six dollars there will be received by the holder ten of the silver tokens at sixty cents each. United States Consuls may likewise be used to facilitate exchanges for foreign holders. The sum of sixty cents is suggested as the new nominal value merely because the bullion has sunk to between fifty cents and sixty cents, and the new rate cannot be less than the bullion value.

Besides the above provisions the law must provide that silver certificates when received by the government shall be cancelled, until the nominal amount of certificates outstanding is reduced to the nominal value of tokens held against them at the new rate. This process will be a redemption of 40 per cent. of the present mass of silver, and there will then be only $330,000,000 in silver tokens, with the same amount of silver as is now behind $550,000,000. The last step will be to redeem the difference between the bullion value of the tokens and the face value at the new rate. With the bullion in each sixty-cent piece worth about fifty-three cents, as at present, the margin for the government to cover will be only about ten per cent. When the amount of certificates has been reduced to the nominal value of the tokens held, the law may provide that on and after a certain day, the silver pieces shall cease to be legal tender for anything above their bullion value, but, that for a limited time, perhaps one year, the government will receive silver certificates and silver tokens at their nominal value, and will give in exchange *one dollar's-worth* of silver bullion for every dollar of nominal value according to the market price at the time ; all silver tokens held or received by the government will be mutilated and treated as bullion, and the great quantity of bullion now in the vaults will be used for these redemption purposes. At the present price of silver, low as it is, there would be enough amply, for the stock is worth about $100,000,000, and the margin for the government to cover would be only ten per cent. of $330,000,000 or $33,000,000. By thus rating the silver dollar pieces at sixty cents each, the ratio in the United States coinage would be changed from the present 16 to 1 into a ratio of 26⅔ to 1. A similar scheme applied to English silver tokens would give a ratio of about 23.8 to 1 ; applied to the French pieces it would give 25⅝ to 1, and to the German pieces about 23½ to 1. It would thus be a long step in the redemption of these silver nuisances.

When the complete redemption has been accomplished,

it will be proper to repeal all legal-tender laws, and, if desired, throw open the mints to the free coinage of silver *without any legal-tender ratio*, but simply on the basis that the silver coins may, when wished, be used at their bullion value, just as gold coins are to-day. It may be objected that this withdrawal of silver certificates and silver tokens will be a contraction of the currency. To say nothing of the many hoards of gold whose owners would be glad to have them profitably employed free of the danger of legal-tender laws, this objection fails to observe that the silver will still be available at its market value, and that there is plenty of silver to be used on such terms. The objection of the mercantile world is not to silver as silver, but to silver as a forced circulation at an arbitrary artificial rate. The above scheme not only removes the dangerous features from the government treasury notes, but provides for getting rid of the utterly unscientific and indigestible mass of forced silver, and is thus applicable not only to the United States but to all countries, as France, that are burdened with legal-tender token silver.

Perhaps some one may argue that if silver were freely coined at its bullion value, the silver standard would result. To this it may be said that since it would be without a legal-tender law, no one would be required to receive the silver for existing debts for more than its worth, and if merchants should happen to find the silver standard more convenient for subsequent transactions, no one could complain. The silver standard is not necessarily in itself objectionable. The objection arises when debts are forced on to that standard at an arbitrary rate. Nor can it be said that the use of two or more metals at rates varying with the market, is at all unnatural. Just such a system arose in England in the last half of the seventeenth century, when the guinea coined by Charles II. to be a twenty-shilling piece was habitually current for twenty-one shillings and over, even up to thirty shillings, when the silver coins were exceptionally bad. A similar system prevails in China, where the metal for large transactions is silver at bullion value, while copper cash for small dealings passes at rates varying with the market. China's system, though clumsy in detail, is based on correct scientific principles, and China has long recognized the idiocy of laws interfering with money.

To reap the best result from the opportunity to use either metal or both at individual choice, no attempt should be made to place a fictitious value on either metal by restricting the coinage. As the act of coinage is merely a verification of weight and fineness, it should be free to all, subject only to a possible charge just sufficient to cover the cost of the operation. A metal cannot fully perform its function as a standard, if its coinage is restricted, for the coins then tend to assume the nature of tokens with a margin of scarcity value over and above the metallic value. The action of India in stopping the free coinage of silver in a silver standard country as a step to a gold standard cannot therefore be considerd sound.

To make a metal a real standard there must be un-obstructed connection between the coin and the bullion, for the coin is merely certified bullion, and there is nothing in the gold standard to make it any more praise-worthy to force a silver country like India arbitrarily to the gold basis, than it is to force a gold country like the United States arbitrarily to the silver basis.

If in the United States the above outlined repeal of legal-tender laws could be accomplished, what a magnificient opening for enterprise the renewed business confidence would give ! Such a result, if once secured, ought to be clinched with a constitutional amendment to prevent backward steps.

IV.

INTERNATIONAL COINAGE.

WHETHER in the world at large a general reform of the present dangerous systems of legal tender can ever be brought about, time alone can tell ; but as a part of such reform, either as a step towards it, or as a final act of polish, the gold coinages of the leading commercial countries ought to be brought into some system of uniformity.

Probably no one will dispute the desirability of having one unit of account and coins based on that unit throughout the leading commercial countries, but many difficulties have been felt in the past in bringing this about. In default of general action, the English Pound Sterling is fast becoming the customary international unit of account, but such custom does not and cannot assimilate coinages. Possibly if the English unit were decimally divided, it would be agreeable to all countries, but hitherto England herself has only *discussed* a decimal arrangement, and has even talked of altering the sovereign or taking another decimal unit gold coin. Consequently other countries have not felt the attractions of the sovereign. Several plans have been proposed,—perhaps the most prominent was one of thirty years ago to adopt five francs in French gold as the unit. The almost fatal objection to this idea is that the French gold coins do not bear a simple relation to the metric weights in which they are expressed, and in which probably any international coins ought to be expressed.

It is hardly to be supposed that any existing national unit will be accepted, unless for very strong reasons, as national pride will be touched. At the same time it will be well if existing units can approximately be easily expressed in the new system, so that for a time, at least, the old national names may continue to be used conveniently, and in fact they *will* continue to be used somehow for some time. The elements of the problem are approximately as follows : A gold coin of convenient size for coinage and for a unit of account, bearing some simple relation to the metric weights, furnishing an opportunity for decimalizing English money without too great violence to conservatism, and offering convenient approximate values for existing national names. The last quality is perhaps of least importance, for the great object is to establish an international unit of account, so that merchants may understand the state of foreign markets at a glance.

While the direct adoption of any one existing national unit would probably not be feasible or desirable, as none fulfills the above problem, still a system derived from an existing unit might be possible. It may seem strange to say that a unit may be derived from the English sovereign so as to meet the above problem quite precisely. Yet such is the case, and the writer ventures to suggest the following as a scheme which he has never seen fully elaborated.

The English sovereign of 20 shillings contains of fine gold 7.32 grammes. Five fourths of this, or 25 shillings will contain of fine gold 9.15 grammes. If the standard fineness for gold is made 915 parts in 1000, a piece of gold of that fineness weighing 10 grammes will contain

9.15 grammes of fine gold, and will equal 25 shillings sterling, or three hundred pence.

The proposition is, that the leading commercial countries shall adopt the standard of 0.915 in fineness for their gold coins, and shall take ten grammes of such standard gold as the unit of account and coinage. Gold coins will be issued of 5, 10, and 20 grammes. One one-hundredth of this unit will equal threepence sterling, and will constitute a convenient sub-unit for retail trade. Threepence sterling contains twelve farthings, so that the conservative Englishman can count for retail sums by threepences of twelve farthings each, instead of by shillings of twelve pence each, and will thus not be deprived of his dearly beloved duodecimal system while acquiring a decimal system for large transactions. In fact the duodecimal system does have certain advantages for fractional purposes, and the retention of a duodecimal step at the end of a system, like a snapper to a whip is entitled to respectful consideration. As the approximate value of the farthing is $\frac{1}{2}$ cent in American money $\frac{1}{2}$ sou in French, $1\frac{1}{4}$ cents in Netherlandish 2 pfennigs in German, and one kopek in Russian, the approximate value of the threepenny sub-unit will be, 6 cents American, 6 sous French, 15 cents Netherlandish, or 24 pfennigs German, and for a time at least it would seem wise to unify this relation, and assign these names respectively to these fractions of the sub-unit, by thus dividing the sub-unit in the different countries. The result will be 1 sub-unit $= 3d = 12$ farthings $= 6$ cents or sous $= 24$ pfennigs, etc. The departure from the decimal scale may provoke opposition outside England, but the departure is only apparent, and need not be permanent. It is only apparent, because with the slightly new values assigned to

the familiar cent, sou, pfennig, etc., will go a correspond-
ing value for the dollar, franc, mark, etc., so that the old
names may be used until the new system is fully adopted
with complete decimalization (outside England of
course).

The method of applying or introducing the new system will require care. Of first importance is the protection of existing debts ; which will be done by providing that in transmuting debts from the old systems to
the new, the amount of fine gold in the old and new
units must control the problem and fix the amount of
new money to be paid.

The following table shows the relations between the
old systems and the proposed one.

COUNTRIES.	Coin or Sum.	Fine Gold Grammes.	Present U. S. Gold Value.	Value in Terms of Proposed Unit.
Scandinavia	24 Kroner	9.677	$6.43	1.0575
Russia, Standard 1896 .	12 Rubles	9.290	6.17	1.015
Great Britain........	25 Shillings	9.15	6.08	1.00
Austria, New Standard, 1894.....	30 Crowns	9.1464	6.078	0.9996
Netherlands..........	15 Guilders	9.072	6.03	0.9914
U. S. A. and Canada..	6 Dollars	9.0279	6.00	0.9866
France	30 Francs }	8.709	5.79	0.9518
Austria, 1867........	12 Gulden }			
Germany.............	24 Marks	8.602	5.72	0.940
Brazil............	10 Milreis gold	8.216	5.46	0.8979
Portugal....	5 Milreis gold	8.128	5.40	0.8883
Egypt...............	1 Pound Egyptian	7.4375	4.94	0.8128
Great Britain	1 Sovereign	7.32	4.866	0.800
Turkey	1 Lira	6.614	4.40	0.7228
Chile, New Standard, 1895........... ...	10 Pesos	5.49	3.65	0.60

In this table, the last column also shows the relation of one dollar, 2 rubles, 4 marks, 4 kroner, 5 francs, 2½ guilders, and 5 Austrian crowns, in gold, to an assumed par of 50 pence sterling.

A troublesome factor in the problem is the disposition of the existing gold pieces, which will not readily fit into any new scheme. In this connection it should be noted that the plan contemplates the use of coins strictly at their bullion value in general, so that in the new system there will therefore be no " least current weight," but all large payments will be verified by full weight. For purposes of large payments in bulk the present coins can be still used with a degree of convenience after allowing for differences of alloy, as these coins will be weighed in large masses. Thus a kilogram of the new standard gold will be equivalent to one hundred of the proposed units of account, and a kilogram of gold of the present U. S. standard will equal ninety-eight and a fraction ; one hundred troy ounces of the new standard will be three hundred and eleven units, and one hundred troy ounces of the present U. S. standard will equal three hundred and five units and a fraction.

It will not, therefore, be necessary to recoin *all* or even the greater part, immediately, of the existing coinage. The only rapid recoining required will be that needed to supply retail trade, where it is desirable to have the coins correspond with the unit of account, as the pieces so largely pass by tale when they are of reasonably good quality. In order to offer an inducement for the withdrawal and recoinage of the old pieces, it will be well to give them a nominal value for future transactions by tale, at something under their real value in the new system, so that it will be profitable to use the pieces of the new system by tale in retail trade, and to reserve the old pieces for payments in bulk by weight where the full value can be used, and for recoining. As a further inducement it will be well to recoin absolutely free of charge whatever the usual practice as to coinage charges may be.

As an example of the course of proceeding in the preceding paragraph, we may take the French Napoleon, which will be worth when of full weight 63.4 sub-units of the new system. A quantity of full-weight Napoleons would be good by weight so that each would cover 63.4 sub-units, but if the Napoleon for tale transactions arising subsequently should be rated at just 63 sub-units, there would be the inducement of 0.4 of a sub-unit on each coin to hold them in large masses for payments by weight, while small tale payments would be more economically made by coins of the new system.

The *approximate values* of some prominent gold coins are in the proposed system as follows :

India	1 Gold Mohur	1.16½
Brazil	10 Milreis, gold	.89½
Portugal	5 " "	.88½
Scandinavia	20 Kroner	.88
U. S. A.	½ Eagle	.82+
Egypt	1 Pound	.81
Mexico	5 Pesos, gold	.80½
England	1 Sovereign	.80
Spain	25 Pesetas, gold	.79
Germany	20 Marks	.78
Chile, Old standard	5 Pesos, gold	.75
" New "	10 " "	.60
Turkey	1 Lira	.72
Austria, 1894	20 Crowns	.666
Netherlands	10 Guilders	.660
France and Latin Un.	20 Francs	.63

Of course the present representative money of notes and tokens will have to be adjusted to the new system. Circulating notes payable in the old system may be exchanged gradually for notes payable in the new system according to the real relation between the two. The tokens may be treated in a variety of ways. They may be called in and recoined, which would be clumsy and expensive. They may be called in and their places filled by a system of fractional notes, as outlined above. They may be called in for temporary notes, and reissued at convenient ratings in the new system, the government taking either profit or loss. They may be deliberately raised to convenient ratings in the new system by a provision that the government will so receive and redeem them and consider that their par value. This last method is the simplest, but the government takes all loss by presenting to the holders the increase in value for which it becomes responsible. Still this would be the best plan to follow with the minor tokens of nickel and bronze, on account of its simplicity. As a general rule, the tokens should not be horizontally lowered in value without a redemption, as this is a repudiation of the government's obligation as to the difference.

The name which the new unit shall bear is of lesser importance. No harm could come from applying a national name to the same coin in different countries, thus the ten gramme unit of 0.915 gold might be called a *Victorian* in England, a *Washington* in America, a *Carnot* in France, a *Kaiser* in Germany, etc.

Here we have a system that answers the problem. A ten gramme coin will be of convenient size for use, and will be an appropriate unit of large value for large transactions, while the hundredth will be a convenient retail

5

unit. For very large transactions one hundred main units, or one kilogram, will offer a good round large-sized unit by weight. The relation to all the metric weights is thus the simplest possible. The English money will be decimalized as to large dealings without entirely depriving it of its cherished peculiarities or destroying the £. s. d. for those conservative Englishmen who may wish to cling to them. The present names of coins will be applied in all chief countries to similar values in simple convenient relation to the international unit.

Some may object to the fineness proposed, namely, 0.915, and desire either the English fineness of 0.916⅔ or the commoner standard of 0.900. If the attainment of fineness in coins were an absolute matter, the convenience of 0.900 might be urged as sufficient, but at best fineness is only a close approximation, and coins of 0.900 in theory may in fact run from 0.898 to 0.902. On the other hand, 0.915 is a more appropriate grade for a decimal system than the endless fraction of 0.916⅔, which is the theoretical English number. The standard of 0.915 has, moreover, one incidental feature which furnishes a link between the metric and English weights. It is this, —34 grammes of the fineness of 0.915 contain, within one-tenth of a grain, one ounce troy of fine metal.

If any of the countries concerned should see fit to test the idea of using two metals, gold and silver, *without a legal ratio*, as was suggested above, it would seem to be well to make the silver system on the same lines as the gold one, namely,—a fineness of 0.915 and coins of 5, 10, and 20 grammes. The unit piece of 10 grammes, or its multiple the kilogram, would furnish the unit for silver transactions, and would seem appropriate for adoption in the silver using countries. The 10 gramme piece would have a similarity to the Indian rupee, and that name rupee, or international rupee, is suggested for it. The Indian rupee would equal one and one sixth of the new rupees of 10 grammes at 0.915, according to fine silver contents.

The matter, however, of an international silver coin, is of less importance than that of the international gold coin, and neither can equal in real importance the solution of the real monetary problem in the world, namely, —the abolition of legal-tender laws : for business can get on with *clumsy* systems of money, but a *vicious* system, that threatens the security of all invested capital, saps the very life of business, and so long as the poison of legal-tender paper and legal-tender silver pollutes a country's monetary system, prosperity must be hindered in a great degree.

V.

SOME HISTORICAL INSTANCES OF LEGAL TENDER.

EVERY country that has a history can show in its own experience cases more or less numerous of debasements of the currency by tampering with the metallic portion arbitrarily, or forcing bad paper into circulation. When a government gets into a tight place, one of its first temptations is to deal fraudulently with its monetary system.

A complete account of the many instances in which governments have debased their money with no regard for existing contractual rights would fill many volumes, but a notice of a few of them and their general course may be of interest here. For a great mass of facts on the history of mediæval and modern money, the reader is referred to Shaw's *History of Currency*, recently published by G. P. Putnam's Sons. A standard special treatise on English monies is Lord Liverpool's *Coins of the Realm*, published first about 1800.

One of the earliest recorded debasements is said to have taken place in ancient Athens under the orders of Solon, though we may well suppose that others before him had performed the trick. While Hannibal was making war in Italy, the Roman money was debased.

The Greek states of antiquity corresponded somewhat in their currency systems. The commonest coin unit was the silver drachma, but different groups of states used different sets of weights, so that the money was not uniform. The Romans may have borrowed their earliest silver coinage system from some debased Greek system, but in the main the Roman coinage was considerably different from the Greek. The chief Roman silver piece analogous to the drachma was the denary or *denarius*, which in early times weighed about 70 grains troy, but by degrees became degraded to the neighborhood of 60 grains in the classical period. As time went on further debasements took place, until in the days of Charles the Great, A.D. 800, it was near enough to 24 grains to be identified with the pennyweight of silver, and as such to form the unit of account in the system then introduced of 240 denaries to the pound. This unit was adopted in England under the name of penny, but to this day the abbreviation for penny is the initial of the Latin *denarius* in the familiar combination £. *s. d.*

The history of the denary on the Continent has been even sadder than that of its English brother ; for while the English penny sank, like the other English denominations, to about one third of its original value, the *denier* or denary of France sank almost out of sight in its infinitesimal obscurity. It became only one seventy eighth of its former self, as did the other French units.

The course of this monetary name unit is typical of many that might be mentioned. One prince or legislature after another continued the debasements till sometimes nothing was left of the coin but its name. As an original question one would suppose that a prince or ruler would wish his country to enjoy the honor of a larger and more dignified unit, rather than a small and contemptible one, but the attractions of plunder have proved irresistible many times.

When Charles the Great established one uniform coinage for his vast domains, he took for his unit the pound of silver, and coined it into 240 denaries, each of which was therefore one pennyweight. Twelve denaries made one solid, and 20 solids made one pound.

After the breaking up of his great empire, monetary confusion ensued. In Germany, particularly, new methods of counting came gradually into use ; especially the systems of guldens and ducats borrowed from Italy. In the lands which afterward became modern France, however, the system of the silver pound continued in use more persistently, though subject to great debasements. By the time of the French revolution, the French pound or *livre* had fallen to about the value of the franc, which was then substituted for it with a decimal subdivision.

In England, Charles the Great's system of the silver pound was early adopted, probably in Saxon times, and the denominations of pounds, shillings, and pence have come down to the present day. The pound that was originally used in weighing silver in England was the *tower pound*, which is fifteen sixteenths of the troy pound. The latter was introduced by Henry VIII. in 1527. The fineness of English silver in the early days was $\frac{37}{40}$. This has been maintained quite constantly, and is to-day the standard sterling fineness.

The original English pound, therefore, was one tower pound weight of sterling silver $\frac{37}{40}$ fine. It speaks well for English self-control that from the days of Charles the Great in the ninth century until the close of the thirteenth century this pound unit was preserved almost intact, and even when debasements had become fashionable they were brought to a close before the unit had been nearly so much degraded as in France. The first debasement of which we have the record was made in the year A.D. 1300 by King Edward I., who debased the unit by 1¼ per cent. This debasement was so slight that it probably was not done for purposes of royal plunder, but was, very likely, a well meant lazy procedure to adapt the new coins to the worn condition of the old ones. It furnished a convenient precedent, however, which was followed by Edward III. three times. Edward III. left only 80 per cent. of the original pound to his successors. Two other debasements occurred in the fifteenth century, and when Henry VIII. succeeded to the throne the unit was down to 53⅓ per cent. Henry VIII. indulged in a perfect debauch in the currency, and Edward VI. continued the same policy. The business of the country got into a terrible state at that time. These two kings not only reduced the weight of the coins, but also tampered with the fineness. Coins were issued as low as $\frac{3}{12}$ fine. There was so much copper in them that they showed red when a little worn.

Finally, in the last year of Edward VI.'s reign, a reform was begun which was continued under Queen Mary and completed under Queen Elizabeth. The unit was raised from its degraded condition, but not to the position it occupied before Henry VIII. began his career. The fineness was, however, under Elizabeth, restored to its ancient standard of $\frac{11}{12}$. The reformed coinage system of Elizabeth, as established in 1560, was a very convenient one. The troy ounce of sterling silver received the coinage denomination of five shillings. This arrangement was to facilitate the verification of coins by weight. The arrangement continued until 1601, when Elizabeth, not content with the excellent coinage system she had established,—with a royal stupidity characteristic of the age, made a slight debasement, and coined the troy ounce of sterling silver into the clumsy sum of 5⅙ shillings.

That was the last legal debasement of England's silver coin. The weight standard of 1601 continued in the coinage of silver till 1817, when the present token silver was introduced. But several propositions for debasement were made in the seventeenth century. The most noteworthy, in the time of William III., is described by Macauley. The heroic exertions of the philosopher Locke and others saved their country from the disgrace of another debasement.

TABLE OF ENGLISH SILVER DEBASEMENTS.

Date.	Fines employed.	No. of pence by tale to a troy pound of sterling silver, 2¼ of lb. of fine silver.	No. of troy penny-weights of fine silver in the nominal pound in money, by tale.	Percentage rela-tion of nominal pound in money by tale, to origi-nal pound in money.
Before 1300 A.D.	3 7/40	256	208.12	100.00
1300 ; Ed. I.	"	559.2	205.56	98.77
1345 ; Ed. III.	"	283.73	187.79	90.23
1347 ; "	"	288	185.00	88.88
1354 ; "	"	320	166.50	80.00
1403 ; H. IV.	"	384	138.75	66⅔
1404 ; Ed. IV.	"	480	111.00	53⅓
1527 ; H. VIII.	"	540	98.67	47.41
Period of Confusion. 1543; H.VIII.	1 8/12	639+	83.35	40.05
1545 ; "	6/12	1065+	50.01	24.03
1546 ; "	4/12	1598+	33.34	16.02
1552 ; Ed. VI.	3/12	3196+	16.67	08.01
1553 ; Ed. VI.	2 21/240	723.25	73.67	35.40
1553 ; Queen Mary	1 1/4	726.54	73.34	35.24
1560 : " Eliz.	3 7/40	720	74.00	35.55
1601 ; " "	"	744	71.61	34.41

The preceding table shows the course of the English silver pound from Edward I. to Elizabeth, according to Lord Liverpool's *Coins of the Realm.*

For a table of the debasement of the Scotch pound see the article "Money" in the *eighth* edition of the *Encyclopedia Britannica.* By the end of the sixteenth century the Scotch silver pound was equal to only twenty English pence.

Gold coins were not largely used in England till the fourteenth century. The first English gold coin of which we have records was issued in 1257. It was called a gold penny, penny being then a general name for any coin. The gold penny weighed twice as much as the silver penny and was legalized as equal to twenty pence. Even at this ratio of about 10:1 there was not enough gold in it, apparently, for the people complained, and it was soon withdrawn. A similar experience met Edward III.'s gold florin in 1345, but in July, 1345, an issue of gold nobles was made which began the series of English gold coins. They were rated at ⅓ of a pound in money, but were equivalent to 1⅛ of the present pound sterling.

The course of the English gold pound unit was generally downward by successive debasements. All three methods were employed, a reduction in weight, a lowering of the fineness, and an increased rating for preceding coins. The ancient fineness was ⅞¹². Henry VIII. introduced the standard of ¹¹⁄₁₂ in 1527 but the two standards were employed concurrently till 1666. The gold pound unit of 1345 contained 408 grains of fine gold, but in 1527 it was only 212 grains. Henry VIII. created confusion in his gold as well as in his silver coins, but in the reform under Queen Mary and Queen Elizabeth a partial return to previous conditions was had. The gold unit was by James I. in 1605 reduced to 141 grains of fine gold, and in 1619 was 128 grains.

All through mediæval and early modern times the English kings were greatly annoyed by the export of gold and silver. This was particularly the case in the first half of the seventeenth century. James I. promulgated the theory that all gold and silver brought into England became a perpetual stock never to be taken out again, and stringent laws were passed, prohibiting the export. The laws were often evaded and the export continued, but occasionally some unlucky merchant was severely punished for his democratic disregard of royal orders. The prevention of this export trade was a powerful motive to induce the kings to debase their coin, or alter the legal ratio from time to time, for by giving the outgoing metal a higher legal valuation, an inducement was made to keep it at home, but it often happened that the king carried his remedy too far, and simply shifted the export trade to the other metal.

In 1666 the guinea was first coined, so called because made of gold from the Guinea Coast in Africa. It was intended to be a twenty-shilling piece, but at the then price of gold was worth more, and generally was current at twenty-one shillings or over. During the period of the great recoinage under William III., when the silver coins had been badly clipped, the guinea sometimes rose to thirty shillings. The legal rate of the guinea was fixed in 1717 at twenty-one shillings, which meant 113 grains of fine gold to the pound, and in 1817 the present sovereign was introduced, containing 113 grains and serving as the pound unit and chief coin. Thus since 1717 the legal definition of the gold pound sterling has remained constant, though worn light-weight gold and irredeema-

ble bank-notes have at times caused trouble. Throughout the eighteenth century the market price of silver
in relation to the mint ratio was generally such as to
leave England practically on the gold standard. The
gold standard has been on the whole the standard of
fact in England since 1700, and in law since 1816.

The following table, from Lord Liverpool's *Coins of
the Realm*, shows the course of English gold coinages in
history.

TABLE OF ENGLISH GOLD COINS.

Date.	Name of Coin	Fineness.	Weight of coin in troy grains.	Legal valuation at date given.	Value in terms of Sovereign.	No. of troy grains of fine gold to nominal money pound.	Value of nominal pound in terms of present sovereign.
1257	Gold Penny	1.000	45	1s. 8d.	£0.08½ 0.393	540	4.770
1345	Florin		108	6s.	= .30 0.950	3.8	3.109
1345, July	Noble	"	136.7	6s. 8d.	.33½ 1.203	4.8	3.610
1347	"	"	128.4	"	" 1.131	383.7	3.395
1354	"	"	120	"	" 1.056	358	3.169
1403	"	"	108	"	" 0.950	322	4.52
1464	"	"	"	8s. 4d.	£0.41¾ 0.950	257.9	2.282
1464, later	Rial Noble	"	120	10s.	.50 1.150		2.112
	Angel	"	80	6s. 8d.	.33½ 0.794	238.7	
1485	Sovereign	"	240	20s.	£1.00 2.112		
	Sovereign	"	240	22s. 6d.	1.25 2.112		
1527	Rial	"	120	11s. 3d.	.56¼ 1.056		1.877
	Angel	"	80	7s. 6d.	.375 0.794	212.4	
	Geo. Noble	"	71½	6s. 8d.	.33½ 0.625		
	Crown	"	57.11	5s.	.25 0.465	210.1	1.859
1543-1553	Confusion						
1551	Old Sovereign of 1527		240	30s.	£1.50 2.112	159.2	1.41 —
	" Rial " "		120	15s.	.75 1.056		
	" Angel " "		80	10s.	.50 0.704		
	New Sovereign		174½	30s.	1.50 1.415	160 —	1.41 +
1601	Angel		71	10s.	.50 0.625	157.2	1.39 +
	Sovereign		172	30s.	1.50 1.394	157.6	
1605	Angel		71	10s.	.50 0.625	141.3	1.25 +
	Unite		154½	20s.	1.00 1.255	141.8	

TABLE OF ENGLISH GOLD COINS (*Continued.*)

Date.	Name of Coin.	Fineness.	Weight of coin in troy grains.	Legal valuation at date given.	Value in terms of present Sovereign.	No. of troy grains fine gold to nominal pound in money.	Value of nominal pound in terms of present sovereign.
1512	Angel	18¾	71	11s. = £ .55	0.625	128.5	1.137
	Unite	22¼	154¾	22s. = 1.10	1.255	128.9	1.140
1613	30s. Piece	18¼	196½	30s. = 1.50	1.727	130.1	1.151
	30s. Piece	"	194	30s. = 1.50	1.707	128.7	
1619	Laurel	22	140½	20s. = 1.00	1.139		} 1.138+
	Double Crown	"	70¼	10s. = .50	0.569	} 128.8	
	Crown	"	35¾	5s. = .25	0.284+		
1666	Guinea	"	129½	20s. = 1.00	1.050	118.7	1.05
1695	"	"	"	26s. = 1.30	"	91.3	0.80
1696	"	"	"	22s. = 1.10	"	108.2	0.954
1717	"	"	"	21s. = 1.05	"	113.	1.000
1817	Sovereign	"	123.3	20s. = 1.00	1.000	113.	1.000
1870	"	"	"	"	"	"	"

The above table seems intricate, but it is simplicity itself beside the coinage histories of some continental lands.

The course of money in the English colonies in America was rather involved. A good account is to be found in Chalmers's *History of Currency in the British Colonies.*

When the colonists first came to America they brought with them the English denominations of pounds, shillings, and pence; but they had little hard cash to fasten these names upon. The little that they got was chiefly Spanish and Portuguese coin, very prevalent in those days because of the importance of the trade with those countries. These coins were legalized by colonial statutes by applying to them an English name in shillings and pence, supposed at first to show their value in sterling money, but as the commerce of the time frequently tended to drain the colonies of money, the colonial governments got into the habit of applying a higher name-value to the pieces than their contents warranted, in the hope that the coins would stay in the colonies. The chief coin was the Spanish silver piece of eight reals ; later called the Spanish dollar. The different colonies applied different denominations to this coin, and from this arose a most confusing series of colonial currencies, long surviving in rural parts where the dollar continued to be called a certain number of shillings ; six in New England and Virginia, eight in New York, and otherwise in other colonies.

The scheme of rating the Spanish coins prevailed also in the British West Indies. From time to time as money became scarce in a colony a new legal-tender act would be passed raising the denomination of the foreign coins and proportionately lowering the colonial standard. Some of these laws, however, provided that existing contracts should not be affected by the new schedule.

In 1652 Massachusetts coined silver pieces of its own at $\frac{3}{4}$ of the English standard. Their reputation for quality was very good and they were very popular in the West Indies. At the beginning of the eighteenth century the English government complained that the colonies were putting too high denominations on foreign silver, and ordered it stopped. The Continental colonies obeyed by adopting paper money. The West Indian colonies adopted a rating of foreign gold which soon gave them a gold standard.

This system of foreign coins rated at various denominations of colonial currency pounds, shillings, and pence continued in The British possession in America well into this century. After the United States began

to coin, its coins were introduced into British colonies
along side the Spanish, Portuguese, and others. Finally
the colonies adopted British Sterling or American
dollars and cents at various times during this century.

Before the change was made the pound currency in
the British provinces north of the U. S. was in the
following condition.

Province.		Value of £ currency in U. S. gold.	Value of £ currency in British gold.	Value of U. S. Eagle in Colonial currency.	Value of Sovereign in Colonial currency.
Newfoundland	Laws of 1845 and 1863	$4.06	16s. 8d.	40s. 3d. Cy.	24s. Cy.
Canada	1841 and 1853	4.00	16s. 5d.	50s. Cy.	24s. 4d. Cy.
New Brunswick	1844 and 1852	"	"	"	"
Nova Scotia	1836 and 1842	3.90	16s.	51s. 3d. Cy.	25s. Cy.
Prince E. I.	1846 and 1870	3.24	13s. 4d.	61s. 3d. Cy.	30s. Cy.

In the West Indies the pound currency was worth in
British sterling from 13s. 4d. in Barbados down to 8s.
in the Windward Islands.

It is interesting to notice that about 1840 Canada gave
the U. S. gold and silver coins a peculiar rating. It
legalized the U. S. gold coins at five shillings to the dollar, but the silver dollars at five shillings and one penny,
which was equivalent to $1.01⅔ in gold. This fact
should be noticed in connection with the rarity of the
silver dollar in the United States before the war.

When the Continental colonies of Great Britain began the use of paper money in the first quarter of the
eighteenth century, they entered on a course which, with
few exceptions, was continued quite extensively till after
the Revolution. The paper was usually over-issued,
irredeemable, and depreciated considerably. During

the Revolution the Continental Congress issued its notes. These were finally of no value whatever. Most of these colonial issues were made legal tender, and as the process continued, a growing disregard of creditor-rights appeared. After the peace in 1783 many of the states were in a deplorable condition, and sought to relieve themselves by still further cheating creditors. All sorts of old goods of small value were pressed on creditors, who were further held off by a series of laws designed to postpone the settlement of debts to the Greek Kalends. Rhode Island particularly attained an unenviable reputation even among her Pharisee neighbors. She was called in derision " Rogues Island."

All these orgies in the currency finally worked a revulsion, and under the Constitution the legal-tender claws of the states were clipped. Congress proceeded under the new powers to provide for a mint. The law of 1792 provided for gold and silver legal-tender coins at a ratio of 15:1. The silver dollar was copied from the worn Spanish dollars then in circulation. Although the law provided for gold coins, too much gold was put into the gold dollar according to the prevailing price, and the country in fact remained on the silver standard where it had before been, so far as the revolutionary paper had allowed it to be on any standard. In 1834 a deliberate change was made, which can be justified on no ground of political morality. The gold coinage was debased about six per cent., so that the gold dollar cut under the silver dollar about two per cent. The ratio of 1834 was 16:1. Its practical result was to establish the gold standard in fact, and the country's metallic standard since has been in fact the gold standard, except so far as the greenback prevented any standard. But whether or not the gold standard was established in the United States by an unjust law, whether twenty or sixty years ago, can be of no concern to-day. The fact that contracts may have been injuriously affected long ago cannot justify attacking existing contracts which have grown up since on the rearranged basis.

The law of 1834 left silver coinage free. In 1853 this was confined to the silver-dollar piece ; and the fractional coins, halves, quarters, and dimes were placed on the footing of government tokens.

During the Civil War the famous greenback legal-tender acts were passed, by which the notes of the United States were made legal tender in private contracts. These laws excited a prodigious amount of discussion, both as to their expediency, and as to their constitutionality. As to their enactment their worst enemies must admit that the men who pushed them through were honest in the belief that they were wise and appropriate laws. Their constitutionality was long discussed, but, unfortunately for commerce, they ran the gauntlet of the Supreme Court. The later acts of legal tender in 1878 and 1890 are too recent in the public mind to need any remarks.

The course of the French coinage was closely analagous to that of the English, only, as before stated, the *livre* or French pound was debased far below the English pound. In the French colonies in America, conditions were similar to those in the English colonies, and similar results were produced. Thus, in 1760, in the French West Indies, it took 150 colonial livres to equal 100 French livres ; in 1805 it took 166⅔ ; and in 1817 it took 180 in Martinique, and 185 in Guadeloupe.

These are only a few of the multitude of cases where

legal-tender laws have been passed ; often with good motives, but finally with harmful results. The cases given will, however, illustrate the principle, and should serve as a warning to the United States or any other country against taking any further plunge into fiat silver or fiat paper.

www.ingramcontent.com/pod-product-compliance
Lightning Source LLC
Chambersburg PA
CBHW031449270326
41930CB00007B/928